WEB COMICS FOR TEENS

MICHAEL DUGGAN

Course Technology PTR

A part of Cengage Learning

COURSE TECHNOLOGY
CENGAGE Learning

Australia • Brazil • Japan • Korea • Mexico • Singapore • Spain • United Kingdom • United States

COURSE TECHNOLOGY
CENGAGE Learning

Web Comics for Teens
Michael Duggan

Publisher and General Manager, Course Technology PTR: Stacy L. Hiquet

Associate Director of Marketing: Sarah Panella

Manager of Editorial Services: Heather Talbot

Marketing Manager: Jordan Casey

Acquisitions Editor: Mitzi Koontz

Project Editor: Kate Shoup

Technical Reviewer: Stefan Szabo

Teen Reviewer: Daniel Vink

PTR Editorial Services Coordinator: Erin Johnson

Copy Editor: Kate Shoup

Interior Layout Tech: ICC Macmillan Inc.

Cover Designer: Mike Tanamachi

Indexer: Broccoli Information Management

Proofreader: Andy Saff

For product information and technology assistance, contact us at **Cengage Learning Customer & Sales Support, 1-800-354-9706**

For permission to use material from this text or product, submit all requests online at **cengage.com/permissions**
Further permissions questions can be emailed to **permissionrequest@cengage.com**

Library of Congress Control Number: 2007939362

ISBN-13: 978-1-59863-467-9

ISBN-10: 1-59863-467-4

Course Technology
25 Thomson Place
Boston, MA 02210
USA

Cengage Learning is a leading provider of customized learning solutions with office locations around the globe, including Singapore, the United Kingdom, Australia, Mexico, Brazil, and Japan. Locate your local office at: **international.cengage.com/region**

Cengage Learning products are represented in Canada by Nelson Education, Ltd.

For your lifelong learning solutions, visit **courseptr.com**

Visit our corporate website at **cengage.com**

Printed in the United States of America
1 2 3 4 5 6 7 11 10 09 08

To Ian and Jephael and every other young soul.
Continue to nurture your nature.

Acknowledgments

Thanks to Esrix, Faith Erin Hicks, James Farr, Jason "Hot Lips" Yungbluth, Robert and Margaret Carspecken, and Sarah Ellerton for the help they gave me; it was wonderful working with every one of them! Thanks to my editors Mitzi Koontz, Kate Shoup, Stefan Szabo, and Daniel Vink for helping me put this book together. Finally, thanks to my family for their continued support. I continue to learn from my mistakes, and without the support of so many people I wouldn't grow from them.

ABOUT THE AUTHOR

Michael Duggan is a writer and artist currently residing in the forests of the Ozark Mountains. He got started drawing cartoons at age three and sold his first gag strip to a local newspaper when he was still in high school. His work has appeared in multiple publications since. Duggan is the author of two books, *The Official Guide to 3D GameStudio* and *Torque for Teens*, both of which he illustrated with his zany characters. He runs the site MDDuggan.com and teaches game design at North Arkansas College. In the personal philosophy of the late Jim Henson, Duggan hopes to leave this world a better place than what it was when he entered it.

CONTENTS

INTRODUCTION

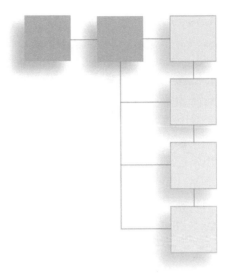

What This Book Is Good For

> True, comics are a popular art, and yes, I believe their primary obligation is to entertain, but comics can go beyond that, and when they do, they move from silliness to significance.

—Bill Watterson, creator of *Calvin & Hobbes*

This book is meant to serve as a basic introduction to a very special type of visual storytelling: web comics. It offers you, the reader, some of the same essential lessons as an art studio or illustration class, graphic-arts or web-design course, or a program in sequential art (i.e. comics). This may be the first instruction you ever receive in creative art or drawing. Even if it isn't, and you hold yourself as a talent in the field of cartoons, this book holds useful nuggets of information and resource links that will come to your aid.

So What Are Web Comics?

Web comics are comics and cartoons published on the World Wide Web for everyone to view. We have all been exposed to pictorial storytelling from a very early age through television, movies, and now digital games and computers. What many don't realize, however, is how much thought and research go into how the succession of images dances in front of our eyes to form narratives. As a cartoonist, I see comics as a unique gateway medium to explore visual narrative. Because comics are such an image-driven medium, drawing is often the skill most emphasized. Therefore, this book will show you both how to draw and how to apply your artistic skills to the comic medium.

Don't worry, though, if you feel you aren't artistically inclined and can't rise above the stick-figure stage. A cartoonist does not have to draw well to be successful. Many of the comic strips that appear in the daily newspapers are proof. One may argue that the drawings of Scott Adams or Cathy Guisewite are charming or quirky, but only the insane would attest to their being "fine art." Drawings don't have to be rendered well to succeed; they just have to be clear and carry a narrative. Certain styles of cartooning are often employed for specific genres. As an example, heroic stories are usually highly detailed and humor is spare. This book will discuss writing gag strips and heroic stories and how best to convey their inimitable narratives.

Not only is the first impression a comic makes upon a reader visual, but a comic's look is, in varying degrees, its content. Artistic style can be a conscious choice that can fluctuate based upon the needs of the story being told and of the artist. Through the exercises in this book you will develop your own artistic style that will set your comics apart from the rest of the chaff you find on the web.

The creation of most commercial comics is broken down into tasks: penciling, inking, writing, coloring, and lettering. Cartoonists must also stage, costume, and add light and shadows to panels to form a vibrant medium. They must research a story and know how to effectively gather visual references to tell it. They must be competent graphic designers, arranging the various elements such as word balloons, captions, figures, and environments in each panel for clarity and desired effect—not to mention know something about fonts and designing layouts. This is actually a lot of work, although these tasks have been made easier with the assistance of computer software. This book will be your guide to getting started in the digital field.

If you desire to make animated cartoons for the web, this book covers that too. Using some of the most affordable 2D animation software on the market, you can put together cartoons to share with your friends and family online. Thrill them, scare them, make them mad, make them laugh . . . whatever your aspiration, you will be able to do it in 2D! The principles, tips, and techniques for Disney-style animation will be demonstrated in-depth so you can start your own personal "cartoon network."

Last but not least, this book helps you get your material published. You will learn what the World Wide Web is, how it operates, and how to carve out your own niche online and get noticed. Techniques for getting people to come to your site and read your comics will be covered. And if you've ever wondered if you could do it all for free, this book shows you how! Plus, this book illustrates how you can start making money with your artwork. All it takes is a little elbow grease and you can become a professional cartoonist!

So if you're ready to start drawing and earn your right to stand beside the comic-art greats at the next Comic-Con convention, then turn the page and switch your information ports to "receive" right now!

From now on, I'll connect the dots my own way.

—Bill Watterson, creator of *Calvin & Hobbes*

CHAPTER 1

So You Want to Be a Comic Artist...

Meet Colleen Doran. She's an illustrator and writer whose published works number in the hundreds. She's worked with big clients, including the Walt Disney Company, Marvel Entertainment, DC Comics, Image Comics, Lucasfilm, and Dark Horse Comics. She has also illustrated the works of Neil Gaiman, Clive Barker, Warren Ellis, Anne Rice, and J. Michael Straczynski. With dozens of large projects going at any given time, Colleen is paid well for her talents. Colleen's career began at the age of 12, when she began writing an epic space opera and fantasy tale called *A Distant Soil*. Since being scouted by a comic-book publisher at a comic-book convention at age 15, Colleen has produced four graphic-novel collections and nearly 40 comics in *A Distant Soil*'s storyline alone. Colleen Doran started her successful comic illustrator profession as a teenager. Although Doran's story sounds fantastic, hers is not the only success story out there.

Many fans of comics—whether they're long-time enthusiasts of cartoons, collectors of comic books, or just regular visitors on Newgrounds.com—dream of one day becoming comic-book artists and creators. Have you ever dreamed what it would be like to create *your* own comic? If you're reading this book, there's an excellent chance that you, like Colleen, would like to be a comic artist. Perhaps you are drawn to the comic medium because of the way it uses words and images together to tell a story in a way no other medium can. Or maybe it's because the materials needed to create a comic, be it paper-based or online, are widely available. Perhaps you're intrigued by the way the Internet enables you to experiment, creating stories that might never be published using traditional means and circulating them in black-and-white or full color—all while remaining incredibly close in the whole creative process. As for me, I believe everyone has a story or joke to tell, and comics in general—and web comics in particular—are a great way to tell it. And when you publish your own web comic, no one can distort your vision.

The fact is, like Colleen, you can create comics if you have the right inspiration and desire. You don't have to wait until you're older or have graduated from art school. There are lots of creative kids, some without a lick of drawing ability, creating their own cartoons and putting them on the web, as you'll soon see.

What This Book Can Teach You

In your hands is a powerful tool—namely, this book, which is meant to be a comprehensive guide to creating your own web comics. Whether you're just starting to draw or have been creating comics for years, this book has something in it for you. Each type of comic is discussed, from short-run comic strips found in school papers to full-length comic-book series to animated cartoons. Plus, this book will show you how to take your production to the next level and put your work on the World Wide Web. The Internet is an amazing place to get noticed and to network with people from all around the world. In this day and age, it's not all that uncommon for a publisher to find your work online, giving you a foot in the doorway at an upscale company where maybe, just maybe, you could wind up making cartoons for a living. If that sounds good to you, then let's get started!

Comics as a Work of Art

Comics are a type of sequential art that often incorporates text in the form of boxes, word balloons, or image captions. As juvenile as some comics may be, they are considered an art form—but because most members of their target audience don't have Ph.D.s, they are a form not often shown in fine art galleries or reviewed by art critics. Because of this, comics are considered a form of "pop art."

The first known comics appeared beginning in the 15th century in the form of pictures that accompanied text to help tell a story. It wasn't until the 1960s and 1970s, however, that the world saw comics' Golden Age. In those days, ne'er-do-wells had much to fear from make-believe superheroes. A comic resurgence started in the 1990s, when computer technology made comic creation easier.

Although comics aren't often viewed as seriously as other types of art, some comics have actually shaped public opinion. In addition, comic-related books—like Art Spiegelman's *Maus: A Survivor's Tale* and Michael Chabon's *The Amazing Adventures of Kavalier & Clay*—have gone on to win the famous Pulitzer Prize, a prestigious literary award. Comics have a unique way of conveying a message, and their stories can be pure fun and cheesy or intricate and deep. If you're going to be a comic artist, it's important that you know that you have the power to influence the very way that people think.

Although scholarly folk typically aren't big fans of comics, this has not stopped them from debating the exact definition and categorization of comics. From those debates we get the following classifications:

■ **Comic strips.** The *comic strip* (see Figure 1.1) is simply a sequence of cartoons that unite to tell a story within that sequence. The term comic strip originally applied to any sequence of cartoons, no matter the length of the sequence or the type of publication, but now the term refers to the strips published in periodicals such as newspapers. These strips are typically satirical strips, like *Peanuts, Hägar the Horrible,* and *Wizard of Id.* In the United States, the term "funny pages" is sometimes used to refer to the page of a newspaper upon which comic strips are found. Most of the comic strips you see in the funny pages are *syndicated,* meaning they appear in many different newpapers.

Figure 1.1
Comic strip.

■ **Comic albums.** Occasionally, when a comic strip is really popular, it will appear as a comic album, which is a collection of published comic strips. You may have seen *Garfield* and *Far Side* anthologies, which contain many comic strips created by the same author.

■ **Comic books.** A *comic book* (see Figure 1.2) is a magazine devoted to sequential art in a narrative form. In the United States, the term comic book has become almost analogous with the superhero tradition, where heroes fight villains across the pages of color art. A certain amount of fandom, including comic-book conventions and marketing events, has elevated some of these comics to cult status in the States.

■ **Graphic novels.** The term *graphic novel* was coined by Richard Kyle in 1964 to distinguish newly translated comic book–type works from Europe from what Kyle perceived as the "juvenile subject matter" so common in the United States' comic books. The term was later popularized when Will

Figure 1.2
Comic book.

Eisner used it on the covers of his trade paperbacks. Technically, a graphic novel is more thematically mature than a traditional comic book and is longer than 100 pages.

- **Manga.** The word *manga* literally translates to *comic* in Japanese. Manga has become huge in the United States, thanks in part to popular cartoons like *Pokemon.* Manga characters (see Figure 1.3) are often kids who wind up on magical adventures with bizarre creatures. Manga has its own defined style and a symbolism based on Japanese culture and tradition. Artists who work in manga are called *mangaka,* and if the printed comics are converted into animation they are called *anime.* Manga popular in the United States at the time of this writing include *3x3 Eyes, Afro Samurai, Cardcaptor Sakura, Cowboy Bebop,* and more.

- **Web comics.** *Web comics,* also known as *online comics,* are comics that are available on the Internet, and run the gamut from traditional comic strips to graphic novels and beyond. Many web comics are published exclusively online; others are published in print but maintain a web archive for commercial reasons. Practically anybody can create his or her own web comic and publish it on the web; indeed, there are currently thousands of web comics available online. Some web comics have even gained cult popularity and commercial success. For instance, *Foamy the Squirrel* of *Ill Will Press* fame has a line of products for sale through Hot Topic stores.

Figure 1.3
Anime.

Web Comics

If you've never read web comics before, you can go online to these sites to get a taste:

- **The Web Comic List (http://www.thewebcomiclist.com).** Over 9,600 web comics listed.

- **Wikipedia's List of Web Comics (http://en.wikipedia.org/wiki/List_ of_webcomics).** Listed in chronological order from 1993 to today.

- **Web Comics Nation (http://www.webcomicsnation.com).** Sorted by category.

- **The Comixpedia List of Web Comics (http://www.comixpedia.org/in-dex.php/List_of_webcomics).** Sorted alphabetically and by category.

- **Keenspot (http://www.keenspot.com).** A web comic hosting site.

- **The Belfry (http://www.belfry.com/comics/).** Sorted alphabetically.

- **The Comic Portal (http://www.thecomicportal.com).** A huge variety.

Spotlight on Esrix

Esrix, whose real name is Tamar Curry, is the creator of the web comic called *Blue Zombie*. *Blue Zombie* (see Figure 1.4) is about a young zombie girl who must cope with everyday life, including being badgered by a videogame-obsessed zombie boy named Gah and pursued by supernatural enemies. Esrix creates the strips with the help of his colleagues John Woodling (a.k.a. Gah) and James Kennedy (a.k.a. Jakal). You can see more of the strips online at entity.comicgen.com.

Q: At what age did you start drawing?

A: I started in the fall of 2002, when I was 17 years old.

Q: What inspires you?

A: I'm inspired by a variety of things: other comics (both on the web and in print), video games, movies, books, music, and even personal friends of mine.

Q: Do you have any tips for beginning artists?

A: Yes, I have several:

- Don't try to be copy cats! Develop your own distinct style of writing and drawing. It's okay to idolize, but imitation can make it harder for you to establish an identity.

Figure 1.4
Blue Zombie #30. (Image courtesy of Esrix 2003.)

- Take the time to plan out your story. It becomes obvious when you start flying by the seat of your pants, as your story (and even your art) will begin to suffer.

- Never lose sight of your original intentions, but never be afraid to try something new at the same time.

- Make sure to keep your readers informed, even if you aren't updating your web pages.

- When starting out, one of the best ways to get viewers is through link exchanges with other web comics. Sometimes even posting a link to another site gets you attention from that site's owners because they check their site's stats to see where people are coming from.

- Which brings me to another point: If you can, be sure to check your site stats to see who is linking to you and where your readers are coming from.

- Seek input from readers and colleagues. They often hold good ideas on a variety of subjects.

- Remember, website maintenance is key! Make sure your site is easy to navigate and that it's easy to find things, that it is not too graphically intense, and that your pages follow the same color scheme/themes with similar objects shared between pages placed in relatively the same area on each page. People will hate me for saying this, but I highly recommend learning at least basic HTML and CSS for maintaining your comic website.

- Leave plenty of time to edit your story before it goes public; the *Blue Zombie* team has been known to do very heavy editing of scripts and even throwing out entire storylines because we didn't think they were good enough!

Q: What's the coolest thing about being a comic artist?

A: The coolest thing about being a comic artist is getting an e-mail from someone who enjoys reading the comic! It is always a pleasure knowing that I did something that entertained someone and made them laugh.

Computers as a Tool to Make Art

With computers appearing in more and more homes and with the growth of computer processing power, there are increasing numbers of examples of comic books or strips where the art is made using computers. Some of these comics mix hand drawings and digital art, while others replace hand drawing altogether with CGI (computer graphic images). Computers are also widely used for both coloring and lettering. Blambot and Comicraft (see Figure 1.5) are two studios that provide digitized fonts specifically for lettering comics.

Because web comics are so new, and because they are, in effect, composites of all the other forms of comic media, this book shows you how to create comic strips, comic books, and graphic novels. This book's focus, however, is on creating web comics. Many self-published comic-book artists have stopped doing print altogether, instead using computers to spread their work. The electronic media of the Internet lends itself well to animation, and several prominent web-comic artists, such as Mark Fiore, have experimented with interaction and animated artwork. Because of this, this book will also show you how to make cartoons for

Figure 1.5
Comicraft supplies comic-book lettering.

the web, called *webtoons*, using 2D animation software. There are several applications designed for this purpose. These programs, and their prices at the time of this writing, are as follow:

- Anime Studio 5 ($49.99)

- Anime Studio Pro 5 ($199.99)

- DigiCel Flipbook Lite ($99)

- Bauhaus Mirage Studio ($395)

- ToonBoom Studio ($399)

- Adobe Flash CS3 ($699)

- Adobe/Macromedia Flash 8 ($699)

You'll find more information about these programs in Chapter 8, "Principles of Animation." Although each application is different, most are similar enough for cross-disciplinary use. Although I use Flash 8 throughout this book, what you learn here should apply reasonably well to any program you choose to use. Note that you will need a computer to perform most of the exercises in this book.

History of Web Comics

Among the earliest online comics were the following:

- *T.H.E. Fox,* published on Compuserve and Quantum Link in 1986

- *Where the Buffalo Roam,* published on FTP and Usenet in 1991

- *Netboy,* published on the web in the summer of 1993

- *Doctor Fun,* published on the web in September of 1993

In the late 1990s, the number of web comics increased dramatically—as observed by Scott McCloud in his treatise on the genre called *Reinventing Comics,* published in August of 2000. Although sometimes controversial, McCloud was one of the first advocates of digital comics and remains an influential figure in the online comics field. Aiding in this growth was Chris Crosby, his mother Teri, and Darren Bleuel, who, in March of 2000, founded the web-comics portal Keenspot, known still for featuring web-comic artists selected for their popularity, talent, or quality.

In addition, Crosby and Bleuel started a free web-comic hosting service in July 2000, originally called KeenSpace but renamed Comic Genesis in July 2005. Indeed, by 2005, web-comics hosting had become a business in its own right with sites such as Joey Manley's Web Comics Nation. Although comic-strip syndicates have been present online since the mid-1990s, traditional comic-book publishers, such as Marvel Comics and Dark Horse Comics, didn't begin making serious digital efforts until 2006 and 2007.

Imagination

When you watch the latest *Star Wars, Lord of the Rings,* or installment of *The Matrix,* what blows you away and keeps you glued to your seat is not the visual effects, the actors, or the sets. What really brings these films to life are the people behind them—the artists with the true creative vision: George Lucas, Peter

Jackson, and the Wachowski Brothers. These people are the ones with the insight, imagination, and sheer drive to bring these motion pictures to life, to give them depth and subtlety.

If you want to make gag strips, you can. But even a gag strip requires an artist with a talent for bringing an artificial world to life—namely, you. Regardless of what type of web comic you decide to create, you are going to face choices about how you do it; how you use your computer and other tools, how you express your story, and how you draw your characters will all capture people's interest. It all depends on you.

You may be bubbling over with an idea for a comic, thinking "This comic's going to be great! It's just like so-and-so's." When you draw it and put it out there, however, your audience will be looking at *you*—not at so-and-so. You need to take credit for what you build. Make something original. Use your imagination. Get inspired. There's no easy formula for success, but if you are drawing what you love and loving what you've drawn, then success will be easier to reach. Don't tear your hair out trying to be somebody you're not. Be yourself. Let your artwork speak for you. You are the auteur of your comic.

Devoting Time to Work

R.K. Milholland of the web comic *Something Positive* recently posted a reply to multiple e-mails about his spelling problems in his comics. He said, "If you are really bothered by my lack of updates or my need of extra proofreading, help me quit my day job so I can devote the time to doing it!"

Most readers of comics just aren't aware of how difficult it is to make and maintain a web comic. What takes less than a minute to read takes hours to create. Strips must be posted, e-mail messages must be answered, the website must be kept up-to-date, and the comic's creator must have free time to be struck by his or her muse.

What's my point? It's this: You might love to draw and want to start your own web comic, but don't expect it to be easy street or immediately net you money. It's a gradual process. It takes time. You have to love drawing. You have to love puttering on the computer, perfecting your drawings and uploading them to the Internet. And you have to do all this without immediate reward. The reward is in the doing. Later, you might get a fan base and publishers beating down your door. Until then, you have to be ready to devote a lot of time to your hard work.

Review

This chapter revealed the many types of comics, as well as offering a glimpse of the history behind comics. You now know that comics are a form of pop art, and that many of them are made using computers. You will soon embark upon the tireless journey of making your best web comics, but first you must look at the basic drawing techniques you should use.

CHAPTER 2

BASIC DRAWING TECHNIQUES

Matisse makes a drawing, then he makes a copy of it. He recopies it five times, ten times, always clarifying the line. He's convinced that the last, the most stripped down, is the best, the purest, the definitive one; and in fact, most of the time, it was the first. In drawing, nothing is better than the first attempt.

—Pablo Picasso

When I went to summer arts camp as a teenager, there were separate teams for music, drama, poetry, and drawing. I was accepted into the drawing team. We came up with this joke as the response for whenever anyone asked who we were: "I am a drawer. Just don't put socks in me!"

The technical term that most people use—artists—did not apply to us. We were grungy dirty drawers. We tromped into the woods with thick sketchpads and came back covered in smudges from our charcoal sticks and markers (as well as in bug bites). We drew nature as we saw it, and we did not consider ourselves artists at all—merely drawers!

Other books will teach you to become a fine artist. This book teaches you the tricks of being a drawer. Your drawings may not look pretty, but they will be yours, and people are going to take notice. In the music industry, there are concert pianists and fine musicians—and then there are rock stars. You are going to become a rock star of the art world.

Psych Yourself Up

I don't want to hear you say, "I just can't draw." We are all born with some basic drawing ability. Every little kid grabs a crayon and attempts to make an image on paper. You may not have used this ability to its fullest potential, but it lies within you nonetheless.

Perhaps somewhere along the way from crayons to adolescence, you became self-conscious about your drawings. Perhaps you had a bad art teacher who harped at you in class, or maybe other kids ridiculed your drawings, or it could be you just lost the urge to draw because you saw other kids who you thought could draw better. There are lots of reasons people stop drawing—but the ability lies inside you still today.

Typically, when someone says "I just can't draw," he really means "I just can't draw like that other guy!" Study your feelings. Are you acting defeatist because you really like someone's artwork but you don't think you can draw like that person can? Let me tell you a little secret: Every artist feels the same way! There are lots of artists I admire and wish I could draw like—but I've never let my inability hold me back. I pick up pencil or pen and attempt to draw anyway. And the more I draw, the better I get at developing my own distinct style—which is more or less equal to those I admire.

Later I'll instruct you to do some research on cartoon styles. When you do, I'm sure you will find some that are sloppier or that look less skilled than your own personal drawing style. When you realize that there are published comic artists out there who draw worse than you do, you'll get an extra burst of positivity. You will realize that not only should you be published, you *can* be published. All it takes is some guts.

Setting Up an Art Studio

Your first order of business is to prepare your own art studio—a private place all to yourself where you can draw to your heart's content, a totally separate place that you go to just to draw. It doesn't have to be a swanky artist's loft or private study; you can easily transform a section of your room or even your desktop into a working studio. The important thing is that it feels like a separate work environment where you go to create, and where you can get in touch with your muse. Your studio needs to be comfortable and inspirational and have proper lighting (see Figure 2.1).

Figure 2.1
A typical art studio.

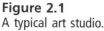

> Be sure to let your parents, siblings, and roommates know that this is your place and that you can't afford distractions when you're working. Distractions are the bane of the artist's existence, and you should develop ways to overcome them without becoming a snarling bear to others.

Every comic artist uses a different combination of art supplies, but some standard ones that you will need are pens, pencils, brushes, and paper. The chief equipment you need to make web comics include the following:

- **Drawing table or desk.** You have to have a proper place to draw. You could draw on a sketchpad you set in your lap or draw lying on the floor, but you'll learn quickly that you don't have the proper range of motion in your drawing arm if you do this. Any kind of flat, sturdy surface will do. (Note that you'll also want a comfy chair with proper back support.)

- **Pencils.** If you made it out of kindergarten successfully, you know what a pencil is and how to sharpen one. But not all pencils are made for drawing. A standard No. 2 pencil will work in a pinch, but you should use real art pencils; they come in varying degrees of hardness. An H on the pencil means that its lead is harder than normal pencils, producing tight concise lines. A B on the pencil means that its lead is softer than normal pencils, producing darker lines and better shading effects. As for the numbers in the classification scheme, the greater the number in front of the H or B, the harder or softer that pencil is; a 3H is not as hard as a 4H and a 4B will be softer than a 2B. My favorite type of pencil for roughs is a 2B—which I always remember as "2B or *not* 2B?"

- **Blue color pencils.** These are used by several industry pros to make soft-tone guidelines and preliminary sketches, which they then ink over. The reason is that the blue won't show up when you make copies of your inked pages on a copy machine. Prismacolor/Col-Erase makes the best blue color pencils.

Note

Later you'll learn how to use a computer instead of blue color pencils for your preliminary sketches.

- **Erasers.** The Pentel Clic eraser is a refillable eraser pen that is great for detail work. You'll also need larger erasers for covering large areas.

- **Pens.** I prefer the Precise fine rolling ball pens, partly because their smooth-flowing ink dries instantly. (I write like a left-handed person, with the side of my palm rubbing the paper, so if the ink doesn't dry quickly I end up smearing ink everywhere.) You can use rolling ball pens, felt-tipped pens, Rapidograph pens (which are slightly more expensive), Pigma pens, crow quills, or calligraphy pens. It's really up to you. If you use a brush, a quill, or calligraphy pens, you'll undoubtedly need to buy separate jars of India ink. ("India ink" isn't a brand name; it's just the blackest ink you can find.)

- **Sharpie pens.** Sharpies are a standard for making thick, strong lines or filling in vast areas of shadow in a picture. Many black magic markers are smelly and slow-drying, or they bleed across the paper, but Sharpie pens are practically dry the minute they're applied. You can get Sharpies with fine or fat tips and in a wide variety of colors.

- **White-out.** Inking your work can be a sticky mess, especially if you draw an entire page of comics, so you will want to use some corrective white-out for making immediate fixes. Carefully dab it where you want and wait for it to dry thoroughly before attempting to draw over it.

- **Rulers.** An all-purpose 12-inch mid-sized hypotenuse triangle will work best, but it should have an inking lip or edge to prevent smearing. I also use a straight ruler composed of bendy plastic so that it always lays flat to the paper, even when I get a crinkle in the pad.

- **Other drawing tools.** Practically any tool you find lying around can be experimented with to create drawings. For example, *Daredevil* artist Alex Maleev uses old toothbrushes to make splatter effects in his work. He dips the toothbrush into India ink and gently flips the bristles with his thumb to splatter tiny droplets across the paper. Similarly, *SpyBoy* artist Pop Mhan sometimes uses Q-tips to ink his comics. Other art supplies that aren't typically used in comics can be employed to great effect, including pastels, coloring pencils, crayons, and magic markers. Many manga artists use charcoal sticks, which are messy and take a while to master, but pictures made with them do seem to breathe a bit more than ink does.

- **Paper.** Bristol board is too expensive (about $10 for 20 sheets), bond paper is too thin, and animation paper is too large. Sketchpads work, but the fancier their covers, the more hesitant I am to put anything in them. Occasionally I pick up a thick pad of newsprint paper, which I typically go through incredibly quickly, but newsprint isn't ideal for drawing comics; it's better for whipping out quick sketches and thumbnail drawings. Heavier (like 50 lb.) bleached white paper is best for drawing comics. Similarly, if you can find them, those glossy white boards that distributors put in the clear plastic baggies with comic books are fun to draw on in addition to being archival (that is, acid-free art surfaces on which ink does not fade with time). The comic industry suggests that full-page comics be drawn on 11 × 14-inch paper—which includes gutters and bleeds—but thanks to scanners and computers, you can make your comics on any size paper and then resize them before printing.

- **Computer hardware and software.** You should definitely get a computer, a scanner, a color printer, and image-editing software. I prefer Adobe Photoshop, but you could use Corel Painter, Jasc PaintShop Pro, or an open-source application such as Gimp or Paint Dot Net (which, by the way, is available on the companion CD). If you want to make animated webtoons, you'll also need animation software, which I'll talk about further in Chapter 8, "Principles of Animation." If you're putting your comics out on the Internet, you'll also need Internet service provided in your studio.

■ **Decorations, snacks, and music.** Make your studio a place you never want to leave. Put posters or artwork by your favorite artists on the walls. Get some music and headphones to listen to tunes while you work. Healthy snacks can help energize a flagging creativity.

For times when you're on the go, you'll want to pick up a satchel, lunch box, tackle box, or other container to assemble a portable version of your art studio. During most of my teen years, I used a grungy-looking old tackle box, which I found in a thrift store, but now I prefer a backpack that I can take with me on long hikes in the woods. Unless you have an easy-to-carry laptop computer and a wand-scanner, your computer equipment probably won't fit into your pack—but then, you shouldn't take such expensive equipment places where it can get broken or stolen anyway.

Sketching and Inking Techniques

This section is targeted at readers who are beginning artists or who have difficulty cartoon drawing. Toward that end, I'll show you the basic sketching and inking techniques that will allow you to wow your friends and family and get you noticed on the Web. These techniques work capably in any medium and are a great place to start.

Before I get to these drawing techniques, however, I want to point out that when you draw, you essentially live on a one-dimensional plane while working in another. That is, you exist in three dimensions, and all the objects surrounding you—this book, the chair on which you're sitting, your computer—are in 3D. When you draw on paper, however, you draw in two dimensions, or 2D. You render 3D objects and people in 2D through the use of lines and values, counting on your audience's eyes to interpret what you draw. This may sound tantamount to magic, but really it's not. When you draw two dots and a curvy line under them, anyone who looks at your image will assume you've drawn a happy face! This *perceptive filter* will be your very best friend as a comic artist.

N o t e

Drawing comics and cartoons *must* be fun. If you have fun drawing, your audience will enjoy reading your strips and looking at your characters. Although it's important to treat this as a serious activity, and although your artwork should continue to grow and progress as you yourself grow and progress as an artist, it's equally important for you to have fun while you work.

Putting Pencil to Paper

The first technique I want to cover is sketching with a pencil. What follows is my way for sketching simple cartoons. It uses simple shapes that you already know how to draw and shows you how to turn them into recognizable characters, and has been proven to work for hundreds of people. For now, I don't want you to worry about making perfect pictures; you're just going to begin sketching. Sketching is something that comes even before you learn to draw. So pick up your pencil and sketchpad and get started.

Note

Pencils—as well as charcoals—have a habit of smudging. Although some artists prefer to smudge pencil or charcoal marks to create washes of gray for shading, which can add to the quality of a drawing, it can fluster even the most experienced artist if it happens when you don't expect it. To reduce smudges, try placing a small piece of paper under your drawing hand (but not covering the area where you're drawing). You can also use spray fixative or hair spray on the paper after you're finished drawing on it, both of which can help preserve your finished masterpieces.

Three Basic Shapes

There are three flat shapes that you will draw over and over in the construction of characters: the circle, square, and rectangle. (Occasionally you might draw a triangle, but as I rarely do I've left it out for now.) Try drawing these three shapes, as shown in Figure 2.2. The circle can be one of the hardest for beginners to draw. Just remember that it's like the square but with the corners whittled off. Plus, your circles don't have to be perfect; you're not an android, after all! As you sketch, avoid gripping your pencil down near the tip or gripping it too tightly; you want your sketching to be loose.

Figure 2.2
The three basic shapes.

Making Them Look Real

These are flat geometric shapes. Your next step is to stretch your imagination and draw them as they'd look in 3D. The easiest way to add depth is to imagine multiple sides to the same shape, some of which you can't see from your viewing angle. The circle becomes a sphere, egg, or cylinder; the square becomes a cube; and the rectangle becomes a long box. Try drawing these shapes, as shown in Figure 2.3.

You might have seen artists draw the cube as in Figure 2.4. What they are doing is drawing two square sides of the cube and connecting them with lines. This makes a transparent cube, like an ice cube, so you can see all the sides. If you want to make the cube appear opaque, you simply erase the lines making up the back side of the cube.

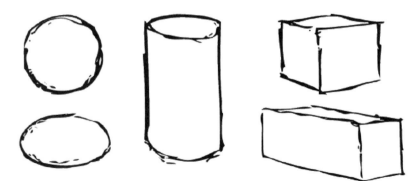

Figure 2.3
The three basic shapes become "real."

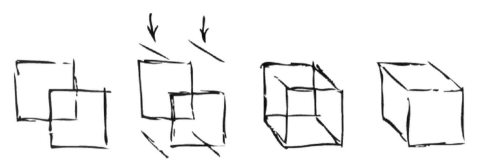

Figure 2.4
Another way to draw a cube.

The easiest way to make shapes appear 3D is to add *values,* such as highlights and shadows. All you need are three values: one for the basic color of the object, one for the highlighted area, and one for the shaded area. Later, depending on your artistic style, you can add graduated tones, which will make the object appear more realistic and less like a cartoon.

To decide placement of the highlights and shadows on an object, you must determine the direction from which the *light source* in a given scene is coming. Most comic artists choose a light source that is off to the left or right of the scene. Highlights appear on objects on the sides closest to and facing the light source, while shadows appear on the same objects on the opposite sides, facing away from the light source. You can also start to simulate volume for your objects by placing shadows on the ground beneath them. Try adding lights and darks to your shapes as in Figure 2.5.

Manipulating These Shapes

Now try to twist these shapes, stretching and squashing them. Imagine that each is made of putty and can be manipulated in many different ways. Remember, however, that all objects have volume and an object cannot show a loss of volume. So even if you show a rubber sphere squashed against the ground, the sphere flattens out at the sides as it becomes thinner in the center—but it doesn't lose its overall volume! Try manipulating your shapes like in Figure 2.6.

Bouncing Balls

Now that you've practiced stretching and squashing shapes, it's worth noting that those two are the most useful manipulations you'll perform with shapes. The

Figure 2.5
Let there be light!

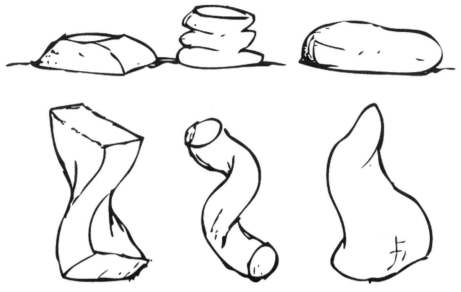

Figure 2.6
Twist, stretch, and squash your shapes.

classic example of cartoon physics is often referred to as "rubber-ball physics"
and if you look at Figure 2.7 you'll see why. Try drawing your sphere bouncing up
and down. Here is where gravity does its thing. The sphere gets squashed as it
comes to a sudden halt upon meeting the ground and pops back up to a stretch
pose as its rubbery composition propels it back up into the arc. The sphere slows
its assent as it reaches to top of each arc, returning roughly back to its normal
shape before continuing to fall.

After you attempt the ball in Figure 2.7, try to use the box or the cylinder in its
place. Make them each look like they're made of rubber. Even better, make them
look like they're alive!

Figure 2.7
Rubber ball physics.

Inking

I've covered the basic techniques of sketching simple shapes; now I want to show you how to ink over your sketch and add value and definition with pens. Inking started out as a way to make pencil drawings show up better for reproduction, and pen and ink is still the most common medium for printed cartoons. For crisp, black lines, or for black-and-white work, inking can make an image really stand out. Pens of various kinds are cartoonists' favorite tools; once you find the one that suits you best, take care so that it lasts longer. That is, keep the cap on your pen when you're not using it so that it doesn't dry out. And if it's a refillable or nub pen, you should wash it and keep its tip from becoming bent.

The outlines of your characters should feature the strongest, boldest lines. They help separate your characters from the background. Interior lines, in contrast, often outline particular details. For shadows, you can draw *hatch lines* or *cross-hatch lines*, which are drawn close together to emulate tonal variations in the picture. Large areas of darkness can be filled in with Sharpie pens or *ink wash* (see Figure 2.8).

Another way to add definition without using hatching is to *stipple*—that is, to add tiny dots of ink. The denser and closer together the dots are, the darker the effect will become (see Figure 2.9).

The space you *don't* draw in is just as important as the part of your picture where you do draw. This space is called *negative space*. And especially when you're inking in lines and details and adding values to your drawing, it's imperative that

Figure 2.8
Hatching and adding ink wash to make shadows.

Figure 2.9
Stippling.

you remember to leave adequate negative space to carry the viewer's eye through your composition. Negative space is also used as a technique to provide you with a more objective artist's eye: by looking at the world around you and seeing the space and distances between shapes and objects, you will draw more clearly and concisely than you would focusing on the shapes and objects by themselves.

Tricks of Perspective

In this section you'll discover how to create a sense of depth or distance in your pictures. This is called drawing in *perspective*. Applying the rules of perspective will help you in everything you draw, but it is most useful in drawing backgrounds for your web comics.

The first basic trick to drawing in perspective is this: The farther away something is, the smaller it looks. For example, the dog in Figure 2.10 is drawn smaller than the cat to make him look farther away. (Note that the dog also appears farther up on the page than the cat; otherwise, it would look tiny in comparison to the cat.)

Another trick to perspective is that parallel lines appear to get closer the farther away they are. In fact, they will almost seem to meet on the horizon. The point where they seem to meet is called the *vanishing point* (see Figure 2.11). When

Figure 2.10
The dog chasing the cat looks smaller in perspective.

Figure 2.11
The vanishing point.

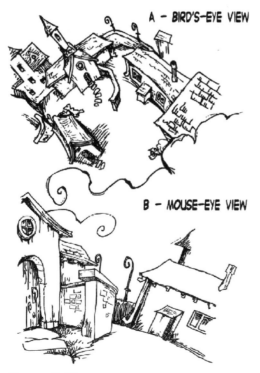

Figure 2.12
The same scene seen from two different angles.

working, make it a habit to sketch guidelines to make sure all the lines in your picture are properly in perspective. If your vanishing point runs off your picture, use your ruler to see where it would be, marking the spot if necessary, so that you can continue your drawing. (You can always rub these guidelines out later.)

A high vanishing point makes it seem as if you are way up high, looking down at the scene. A low vanishing point makes it look like you're on the ground looking up at the scene. In this way, you can draw pictures from a bird's-eye view or a mouse-eye view (see Figure 2.12).

Related to these viewpoints is *foreshortening*. When you look at an object, like the maniacal clown in Figure 2.13, the part that is closest to you will appear larger than the parts of the clown's body that are farther away. Using alternate viewpoints like this can make an ordinary picture look quite dramatic. To get the hang of foreshortening, try drawing this clown. To begin, draw a set of guidelines fanning out from a central point near his feet and then fit the clown roughly between the guidelines.

Figure 2.13
A maniacal clown seen from a bird's-eye view.

Figure 2.14
A country road in perspective.

You can convey different levels of depth by making shapes and colors less distinct the farther away they are, adding detail to only those shapes that are nearest to the viewer. Lines going across as well as back in a picture can also add depth, as in Figure 2.14. (Notice how the road gets narrower in perspective as it gets farther away.)

Review

In this chapter you learned the basic techniques behind drawing, including drawing in perspective. You explored how to make shapes look 3D and how to use a variety of art tools. You will use these same techniques as you continue through the rest of this book. I recommend that you attempt to copy the illustrations in this chapter as an exercise, and to draw as much as you can in your free time so that you become the very best drawer you can be—and no, I won't put socks in you! In the next chapter, you will learn how to draw characters.

CHAPTER 3

CHARACTER CONSTRUCTION

Backgrounds are cool, but when you read a comic or watch a cartoon, the background and other objects in it are not what you pay attention to. What you—and other readers like you—*really* eyeball in a cartoon are the characters, their antics, and their conversation. That means, then, that to be a web-comic artist you must be able to draw great characters. Your characters have to be immediately compelling and keep your readers' attention.

Creating Memorable Characters

SpongeBob SquarePants. Homer Simpson. Ren and Stimpy. Snoopy. Garfield. Teenage Mutant Ninja Turtles. Their names evoke memories and feelings. All these characters, plus so many more, have become truly memorable in their own right. They transcend the line drawings and color compositions to become popular icons. Sometimes a character seems to become a legend overnight, but in fact, it is the struggle and vision of its creators that lead to a character's ultimate success. No character starts fully formed.

First, artists sit down and brainstorm character ideas. Then character concept sketches are drawn. Amid countless variations, a single sketch will be chosen and launched into full-fledged character model sheets. Digital artists then perform color comparisons and editing. Finally, a character is born.

Character Traits

Creating a memorable character—one that people want to watch over and over again—is rewarding. One of the integral parts of a character's appeal is his personality. Character traits are vitally important because they shape the character's looks, actions, and dialogue. All the most successful cartoon characters have well-defined (as opposed to wishy-washy) personalities. For example, Bugs Bunny is a wisecracking carrot-chomping rabbit with a knack for talking his way out of situations. SpongeBob SquarePants is an affable and perky yellow sponge who never lets life get him down.

Before you plunge into drawing your comic characters, you should make sure you have defined for that character at least three distinct traits and skills. By giving your characters traits, you can immediately see how the character would interact with others. This forms the character's behavior and the sorts of choices he will make.

Whatever you do, do not choose boring or agreeable traits. For instance, you may make a Prince Charming hero who is brave, dashing, and good-looking, but these traits shape him into a bore; add the trait ''clumsy'' to that list, however, and you have a funny and likeable character!

Names

Another element that should be obvious when we talk about character appeal is the character's name. The Renaissance painters Raphael, Donatello, Leonardo, and Michelangelo are not nearly as well-known by the public as the Teenage Mutant Ninja Turtles with those same names. So far, there haven't been any popular cartoon characters who go totally nameless. Your character's name is really important, as it reflects the character's personality.

The choice of a name should not be made lightly. It influences how the reader reacts to and interprets the character. If you name a character Melvin Moregood, your reader has some idea that the character is a nerd without even having seen a drawing of it. On the other hand, if you name the character Smash Freely, the reader knows the character will probably be a big thug of a guy. Don't overuse comically obvious nomenclature like this, but definitely give the names you invent some thought.

Tip

To help you pinpoint the perfect name for your character, check out a baby-name book from your local library. Those are the books that expectant parents use to choose the names of their offspring. These books provide tons of information about names and how they will be received by others. I've used baby name books many times when I needed to find just the right name for a character.

Appearance

After you have decided on a character's personality and name, you can focus on how the character will look. Do several thumbnails of your character before you make the final decision on what he or she will look like. *Thumbnails* are smaller sketches that cover the salient points concisely without any real details. Fill one or more pages with thumbnails; then squint at them to see which one leaps off the page. If squinting doesn't work, put the thumbnails away for a day or two; when you look at them again, one of the images may call to you more than the rest.

Choose the strongest and most impressionable image for your character, and then sit down and get busy drawing. First do a full-featured drawing; after that, draw a model sheet. *Model sheets* depict the same character from multiple angles, in multiple poses, and with multiple expressions—in other words, in as many varieties as possible (see Figure 3.1). Model sheets help not only you when you're drawing, but also when other artists work with you to complete a comic.

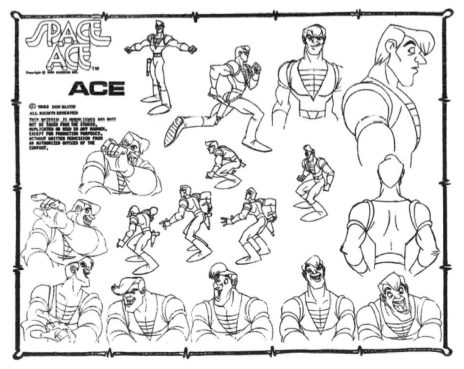

Figure 3.1
Model sheet for Ace in *Space Ace*. (Image courtesy of Don Bluth Productions 1983.)

Making Your Character Come to Life

Using just basic shapes, you can draw any character you can dream of. The following techniques show you how to make lines on paper look like somebody. The simple pencil shapes I show you here are just a framework on which to build your characters. Once you've mastered the basic "skeleton" of character creation, you can create endless variations to people all your cartoons. After all, most humans have the same basic shape, although no two of us are exactly alike. As you get more confident as an artist, you'll be able to change the shapes and add in all kinds of stylistic details that will really bring your characters to life.

Bringing an Object to Life

Take the sphere and the cube and put them together for a soft doughy shape, which we'll pretend is a pillow for now. The pillow can bend, twist, and bounce just like the other shapes you've practiced. Now imagine that it has tails coming off each of its four corners. The two tails touching the ground can be interpreted as its feet, and the two tails that are up in the air can be interpreted as its hands. You should keep your shape loose and organic. Making something that's not human look like it has human traits is called *anthropomorphizing*. By anthropomorphizing this rudimentary shape, you are doing what countless Disney artists have done before. It's a very popular exercise, and it will teach you a lot about proportion and character movement. Attempt this exercise, which is illustrated for you in Figure 3.2.

Note

When you look at a cartoon artist's work, what you are really seeing is the final polished product. There's no telling how much preliminary work it took for the artist to get to that stage. So don't worry if it takes you time getting from a basic character to a fully realized cartoon character.

Figure 3.2
Give the pillow "life."

Bringing People to Life

Draw the same pillow you worked on before—but with limbs attached to the corners of the pillow and a head popping out on a neck in the middle of the top, in between the arms (see Figure 3.3). The limbs—both the arms and the legs—should each seem to be made up of a single cylinder. When they bend, however, they should look like two locking cylinders. The head is basically a sphere with details added on to it. (I'll get to the particulars in a bit.) Characters are normally about seven heads high, but the exact number of heads varies depending on how cartoon-y you want your character to look. (In art terms, one "head" is the length of someone's head.)

Note

If you're a self-taught cartoonist, you may find that building a character in this manner seems difficult or even a little childish, but I want you to give it a try nonetheless. This type of drawing helps improve your proportions when drawing from live models, and it will seriously help when you do animation.

Body shape can let a person know a lot about a character, especially gender, strength, how much they work out, and more. Men have a larger rib cage and torso, while women have larger pelvises. People know what people look like, so if the body you draw looks odd, people are going to notice; take a look at Figure 3.4

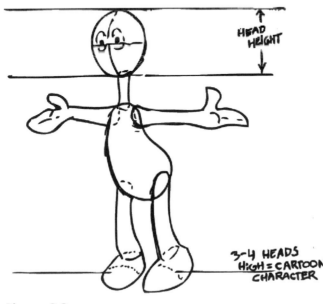

HEAD HEIGHT

3-4 HEADS HIGH = CARTOON CHARACTER

Figure 3.3
Add limbs and a head to make a basic character.

Figure 3.4
Varieties of bodies demonstrate gender and build.

for some other bodies. As you can see, you'll probably use the basic character construction setup for most cartoon characters, individual style aside.

You can morph this basic construction setup in many different ways to create a cast of thousands. For instance, you can elongate the torso and limbs to make a taller character and give him a square head—as A shows in Figure 3.5—or you can squash the torso and make the limbs short little spheres, like B in Figure 3.5. These endless variations, when placed into your comics, will make your characters more compelling.

Making Faces

As mentioned, the head should be a sphere. It doesn't have to be a completely round sphere, like Charles Schulz's Charlie Brown character. You could make it an egg-shape, a soft square, or even add another semi-circle at the bottom front of it for a jaw like you see in Figure 3.6. To draw your character's face, very carefully draw two faint pencil lines across the head; these will be your guidelines. The nose

Figure 3.5
Variations in character construction.

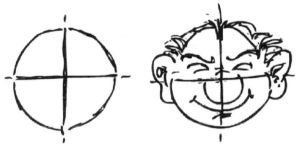

Figure 3.6
Making the face.

goes on the front, where the two lines intersect, the mouth goes just underneath, and the eyes go slightly above the nose. (On real people they go about an eye's width apart from one another, but on cartoon characters they can go almost anywhere.) The ears are level with the eyes. When you're finished, erase the guidelines you drew on the face. Optionally, add hair or a hat for individuality.

Drawing Eyes

It's commonly said that eyes are the window to the soul. Indeed, eyes and eyebrows are among the most expressive elements of characters, and can set one character's appearance apart from another's. Eyes are as diverse as people—perhaps even more so in the web-comics universe. In comics, good guys, small children, *chibis,* and cute fuzzy things tend to have large eyes with wide pupils (the dark center of the eye) and very thin eyebrows. In contrast, bad guys and shifty characters in web comics often have narrower eyes and big bushy eyebrows. The size, slope, and contour of the eyes add a lot of character to people, as do the shape and thickness of the eyebrows. For instance, eyebrows that rise up on the ends just above the bridge of the nose can indicate surprise, shock, interest, or curiosity, but if they slope down in a sharp V over the nose, eyebrows can indicate anger or even fury.

Note

Chibis are cute little people drawn in Japanese comics. "Chibi" literally translates to "tiny"; as such, chibis are child-like, with tiny bodies, big heads, big eyes, and small mouths.

The eyeball itself is normally a sphere that sits in the eye socket of the skull. (You can learn about the muscles, aqueous humor, and other components of the eye in any biology book.) The eye's iris is the colored part of the eye; it normally has bands of multiple hues and lines radiating out from the pupil, like the spokes on a bicycle wheel. The pupil is round but changes size, generally due to ambient lighting or emotional response. (Of course, in comics, characters need not have round pupils. Cartoonist Johnen Vasquez usually draws his characters with square pupils. Cats and demon characters typically have slits. Figure 3.7 show some examples of eyes from comics I've read. As you can see, styles can vary greatly.

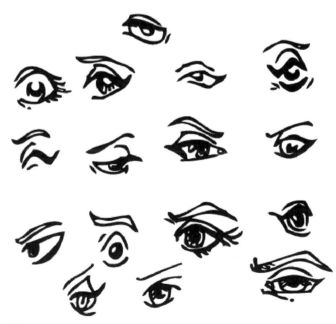

Figure 3.7
Different styles of eyes.

Tip

A lot of artists have a biology book or two in their libraries. It never hurts to have one around when you need to get a fix on human anatomy for a drawing.

Drawing Noses and Mouths

As a structure made of cartilage that can come in all shapes, the nose can be insufferably difficult to draw. Some artists opt to draw a dot or a dash for a nose. Others, such as manga makers, often draw a straight vertical line with a divot for the tip. Older cartoonists in the tradition of *Ziggy* make the nose a big bulb between the eyes. Some comic artists don't even draw noses at all. Seriously, if noses aren't your style, you don't even have to mess with them. But if you do, get creative.

You have just as much freedom when it comes to lips and mouths, but keep in mind that they can express tons of emotion, from an O of fright to a shout of joy, and they move around a lot. They can be drawn simply, as a solid line, or highly detailed. It's up to you and depends on your personal style, which I'll talk more about in Chapter 4, "Express Yourself."

A general rule of thumb is to focus on having a top and bottom lip. The bottom lip tends to be larger than the top. Men's lips tend to be thinner than women's, and they are typically drawn as two lines—one to indicate where the lips meet, and one for the shadow under the bottom lip. Fuller lips tend to signify that the character's a woman, which can be drawn by outlining the upper and lower lips or by making the bottom lip's line a bit fuller and rounder.

When the mouth is open, some teeth typically show. You can draw teeth as just a white space, you can sketch each tooth separately, or you can draw something in between these two styles. The tongue sometimes shows if the mouth is open enough; if so, the tongue is triangular shaped.

Figure 3.8 has some noses and mouths as examples from comics I've read. Styles can vary greatly.

Looking Around

In the section "Making Faces" earlier in this chapter, I mentioned that guidelines should be used to determine the placement of the eyes, nose, ears, and mouth. Assuming the character is facing forward, the lines should be roughly centered on the head. If the character's face is being viewed from an angle, however, the placement of these guidelines changes.

Figure 3.8
Different styles of noses and mouths.

The image labeled A in Figure 3.9 shows a face from the front view, with the guidelines crossing it. As the face turns to look to the side, the horizontal line across the face stays where it is; the vertical line, however, curves to one side. (If you have trouble imagining this, find a basketball and look at the lines on it,

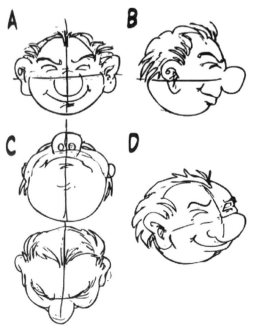

Figure 3.9
Drawing the face from different angles.

noticing how they shift when you slowly turn the ball.) The image labeled B in Figure 3.9 is a side view, or profile shot. Here, the vertical guideline disappears altogether, but you still have a line across the middle to show you where the nose and ears should go. To draw a face that is looking up or down, the horizontal line must curve, with the facial features following suit, as shown in the image labeled C in Figure 3.9. The hardest angle to draw any face is shown in image labeled D in Figure 3.9. Can you see how both the guidelines are curved? (Note that as you move the facial features around to follow your guidelines, they should contour around the cranial sphere.)

Two types of faces always look a little different: those of the young and those of the elderly—although the eyes stay the same no matter how young or old the person is. Very small babies seem to have big eyes, but it's really just that the same eyes they'll have as adults are set in a very tiny face.

People's faces stop growing as they mature—except for the nose and ears, which keep growing for the rest of your life. The older the person, the larger the nose and ears will look in comparison with the remainder of the face. People get wrinkles, too, mostly from showing the same emotion again and again. Common spots for wrinkles are around the lips and the corners of the eyes, although they can also show up on the forehead and between the eyebrows. Additionally, the skin starts to hang differently off the body from years of gravity—most noticeably around the chin and under the eyes.

Little kids are different, too—they have round heads that are big relative to their bodies, and their bodies appear more rounded, because of what is called "baby fat," which goes away as they get older. Kids have small unformed lips, button noses, and missing teeth, all of which help to shape their faces.

Adding Hands and Feet

Cartoon hands and feet, like cartoon heads, are larger than on a real person. You can cheat when drawing hands and feet. In the next chapter I'll show you more characteristic ways to draw them; for now, try making hands by drawing long ovals and sticking thumbs onto them (see Figure 3.10). Don't worry about making individual fingers for now. Feet can be made of one, two, or three ovals joined to the legs. This will do until you decide on your own style.

You might notice that some cartoon characters have fewer fingers than human beings should. This is not a mistake. This convention has its roots in animation

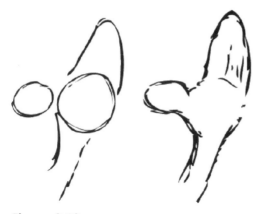

Figure 3.10
Making simple hands and feet.

simply because it was easier for the artists to paint and animate only a few fingers conservatively, but it also helps prevent drawers from making their characters' hands look like bunches of bananas. You decide how many fingers your characters will have.

Adding Hair

Most artists really like drawing hair. Just like we humans fuss with our own hair and show our individuality in the ways that we wear it, so too do we like to draw hair on our characters. (Of course, our characters could be bald, but this section focuses on hirsute characters.) Hairstyles in web comics can be of any color and length, and you rarely see a "bad hair day." Hair can be an extension of personality.

I normally lightly block out hair while I am sketching. Then I draw some strands of hair, in clumps and groups, since this is how hair typically behaves on people. I outline the hair or, if I feel like it, I merely draw in some quick dash lines. When drawing hair in black and white, the more lines in the hair, the darker it appears. Blondes have hardly any shading. Redheads and brunettes have a medium amount.

Hair is not plastered right to the skull. Instead, it has volume and life. Most folks have a part in their hair, either on a side or in the middle. People arrange their hair countless ways, including cut, dyed, permed, and styled. Be creative, or look at magazines or books for inspiration.

Adding Clothes

Humans are the rare mammals that actually wear clothing. Although clothing is worn primarily for protection, modesty, and warmth, another major reason people wear clothing is for individual expression. Characters can show their personality in their clothing and in the way they wear their clothing. Clothing can alter perceptions of a person, instantly giving away clues about his or her personality, taste, socio-economic class, and whether he or she belongs to a group or occupation. It can also be used to convey visual interest.

Although you can place different clothes on the same figure to radically change your reader's perception of the same character, most cartoon characters wear the same clothes in every strip in which they appear, partly for immediate recognition (the outfit becomes a signature costume) and partly so that our perception of the character doesn't change. Thinking of the clothing you are going to draw can be difficult, but it can also be a lot of fun. Peruse costume books, fashion magazines, and even your own wardrobe for inspiration. Just observe and draw as much as you can; as a last resort, put your characters in your own clothing.

Whatever type of clothing you choose for your character, remember that clothing has volume and weight, even if it is only a light-weight fabric like silk. All fabrics wrinkle, even the skintight ones. It's hard to figure out just where to place the wrinkles, but they are generally where joints and bends are, such as the inside of the elbows and knees, and where clothing is tucked in or folded over a part of the body. Remember that the heavier the fabric's material, the thicker the wrinkles will be.

Bringing Creatures to Life

You can draw animals and other nonhumans in a similar way to drawing people: by using simple shapes and guidelines and adding features afterward (see Figure 3.11). Creatures make good cartoon characters, too, because you can use their natural physical characteristics—such as tails, ears, noses, and claws—to great effect. You should probably use a photograph of an animal as a reference when drawing so that you get the proportions and anatomy right. If you're drawing a mythical or fantastical creature, you should use a combination of artist renditions of that type of creature and photographs of animals that come close. For instance, if you're drawing dragons, use paintings by Keith Parkinson (or other dragon artists) along with photos of crocodiles, iguanas, and bats.

Figure 3.11
Drawing a dragon.

There's a type of cartoon drawing called a *furry*, where normal human characters are replaced with anthropomorphic animals in mature stories (see Figure 3.12). This comes from furry fandom, which started at a science-fiction convention in 1980. This fandom is distinguished by its enjoyment of humanoid animal characters. Examples of furries include the attribution to animals of human intelligence, facial expressions, anatomy, speech, walking on two legs, and the wearing of clothes.

Figure 3.12
Furry characters of *Faux Pas*. (Image courtesy R & M Creative Endeavors, 2001–2007.)

Spotlight On Robert and Margaret Carspecken, The OzFoxes

Robert and Margaret Carspecken are a husband-and-wife team that run R & M Creative Endeavors. They have been working together since the age of the dinosaurs. They do comics and cartoon art, wildlife paintings, children's books, cookbooks, greeting cards, t-shirts, collectable prints...pretty much whatever attracts their interest and seems right for the art and stories they want to tell. In the world of comics they are best known for their web comic *Faux Pas* (see Figure 3.13); for the illustrated cookbook *Sweet Treats*; and for their comics/convention-oriented illustrations using animals as the central characters.

Q: At what age did you start drawing?

A: We both started at an early age, four or five, mostly drawing animals: horses, deer, rabbits, cartoon characters from TV and movies...that sort of thing.

Q: What inspires you?

A: Well-told stories using art, whether it's illustrated text (like children's books), comic books, comic strips, animation, even single works of illustration. Art has the potential to tell an unlimited number of inspiring or informative stories, and we appreciate well-crafted art in all its forms: movies, comics, book covers, paintings...whatever.

Q: Do you have any tips for beginning artists?

A: Three biggies:

- First: Talent is good, but perseverance is better. There is no substitute for practice, and the more you work at it, the better you'll get. It's important to figure out what you like (and, eventually, why you like it). And learning from others is great, but all the planning in the world won't help you produce better art. Applying pencil to paper, brush to canvas, stylus to tablet...that is where improvement comes from.

- Second, and just as important: Learn the craft of storytelling. Art will attract attention, but it's writing that keeps an audience coming back. Look at your favorite movie, comic,

Figure 3.13
The OzFoxes' *Faux Pas*. (Image courtesy R & M Creative Endeavors, 2001–2007.)

or painting, and try to figure out how the creator(s) made it so interesting. Comics can be exciting, informative, daring, funny…but if they're boring or badly told, no one will come back for more. A good story can carry bad art, but even great art won't hold an audience if the storytelling is bad, so learn how to tell a good story!

■ Third: Enjoy what you do, and do it because you enjoy it! If you are merely cranking out comics because it's something to do, that lack of enthusiasm will make your comics dull and uninteresting. Share your best because you care and because you love doing it. You and your audience will be happier for it.

Q: What's the coolest thing about being a comic artist?

A: There are so many things! First of all, comic art reaches people at a level that is generally non-threatening, meaning it's a great way to entertain and share your ideas. If you do it well, comics can make it possible to meet people you would never meet otherwise and you realize just how many people out there share your interests and enthusiasms. You can work on comic art anywhere, anytime, so long as you have a pencil and a scrap of paper. You can tell any size story you want, from small personal stories that span a few moments to colossal epics that roam all of time and space. If you are doing your own comics, the final results are completely under your control, which is both exciting and a little scary until you get used to it. Best of all, comics are unlimited: you can be humorous, you can be thought-provoking, you can tell exciting stories, you can show people how to use a fire extinguisher…the only limits are your dedication to your craft and your imagination. In comics, what you do is up to you!

Review

Now that you know how to create characters, take some time to practice the techniques discussed here. Fill a sketchpad or notebook with characters and character ideas. You never know when you will need an original character in a pinch, and your early doodles may just save your butt someday. The next chapter looks at creating your own personal drawing style, which will help you jump out and be noticed.

CHAPTER 4

EXPRESS YOURSELF

If you can draw at all, you have a great gift—one that should not be stifled by your trying to be someone else. If you spend all your time and energy trying to be like your favorite artist, you'll come off to the public like a wannabe. People respond to originality. No one loved listening to Elvis Presley or called him the King of Rock-n-Roll because he sounded just like every other singer. They respected him because he was different! Everyone has their own unique art style (whether you know it yet or not), and it's this original style that people will buy into. It's what will make you famous.

In this chapter, I want you to be different. The one thing that makes an artist's work stand out from the crowd is his or her individual style. All the cartoonists who have really made it big have very distinctive and memorable styles, which none of their imitators can quite match. You will develop just such a style. Try different art styles, try what other artists have tried before, experiment with drawing different character types, and learn what it is that will set you apart from all the other comic artists out there today and what will make you a star.

Tip

Draw big pictures. Most comics are printed smaller than the original drawings. Drawing bigger pictures gives you more room to add all the details.

Copying Other Artists' Styles

You may or may not feel guilty about copying. It is certainly wrong to attempt to copy someone else's hard work and pass it off as your own. This is why there are copyright laws that protect artistic endeavors in this country. But as many a "self-taught" artist will tell you, copying another artist's style can be the first real step in learning.

You should begin by copying a cartoon figure from an artist's work you admire. Some of the first cartoons I ever drew as a child, when I was about three years old, were of Charlie Brown, Snoopy, Garfield, and the Pink Panther. The first time I read a *MAD Magazine,* I sequestered myself away on the playground every afternoon copying the strips from its pages.

Take a look at the differences in the art styles between A and B in Figure 4.1. These are just two examples of a wide variety of comic art. You can find more variety online at http://www.comics.com, in your newspaper, or at your local comic-book store. There are also several web-comic lists online that can help you find more web comics to look at. I mentioned some of them in Chapter 1, "So You Want to Be a Comic Artist . . . ."

Practice with a wide variety of cartoon art styles. While copying someone's drawings, put yourself into that artist's shoes. How did the artist think to put his or her characters together? What are the basic shapes from which the artist's figures are made? Finally, try combining what you learned from what one artist did with what you learned from what another artist did. When you start putting all the pieces together and you decide what you want to use in your own work and what you don't, you are starting down the road to your own original art style. The more artists you learn from, the more individual your own personal style will become.

Do you still feel guilty about copying? Let me point out that all artists' styles are a mixture of all the things they learned from the artists they admired and who have gone before them. When and if you go to art school, you will learn under a professional artist who will teach you his or her way of drawing. It's the unique way in which all these ingredients are blended together that creates the artist's bread.

Developing Your Own Personal Look

The first thing to do, after studying other artists' styles, is to take a firm survey of your own work. Pick out your very best artwork and study it for a while. Are there visual trademarks that you use? Is there one type of eye, nose, or ear you gravitate

Figure 4.1
Two examples of comic art style: *Demonology* (image courtesy Faith Erin Hicks, 2007) and *Inverloch* (image courtesy Sarah Ellerton 2007).

toward again and again? Does your medium work well for you? Are your characters compelling, friendly, and/or funny? Are there any other features about your work that seem to speak to you? By that same token, are there any that you're consistently displeased with or that you'd like to erase?

Tip

Stop worrying about drawing a "perfect" picture. Often mistakes can make your cartoons look funnier or more individual than you originally intended.

After doing a personal survey, you might want to hazard something even more daunting: having your closest friends or people who share your interests critically evaluate your artwork. Although no one in their right mind enjoys criticism, constructive advice can be very useful. Keep in mind that there are always different strokes for different folks, and people can have entirely opposing opinions of what's good and bad—especially when it comes to art. Listen to every bit of advice, even if you don't agree with it, remembering that the decision about what you're going to do with your work is yours.

Every comic artist has undergone this process of evaluation and change. For inspiration, try to find early examples of the work of your favorite cartoonists to see how their work has progressed and changed over the years. Progression is key. Find what works and discard what doesn't, understanding that some things will work for you that don't for another artist and vice versa. And don't get locked into one style, expecting to never change, because your drawing should always show improvement.

Facial Expressions and Body Language

Visitors to your web comic may respond well to your lines and color choices, but it's really your characters that will express your vision the best—through facial expressions and body language.

Facial Expressions

Drawing facial expressions can be one of the most terrifying challenges for new artists. We look at faces every day; indeed faces are what we focus on the most when trying to understand someone else's emotions. But despite this familiarity, this makes drawing faces a challenging task—that is, people are so adept at reading faces that you must render them just so in order to convey your meaning. There are some easy techniques to make it less challenging, however. Indeed, by making very simple changes to a basic face, you can portray a wide range of facial expressions.

Most expressions are universal. If you were from San Diego, California, and found your airplane crash-landed somewhere in Russia, you would still understand if a native smiled at you that he probably wanted to be friendly. If you know the facial expression you are trying to draw, chances are good your audience will recognize it. For example, a down-turned mouth and eyebrows drawn together in a V would make most people think the character is angry.

To develop your face-drawing skills, set up a mirror in front of your work station and use it anytime you need to see how a facial expression should look (or what other parts of the body do in a specific pose). Another option is to record yourself using a digital camcorder and play it back frame-by-frame on your computer.

Because you are drawing a web comic, you are not hampered by having to draw realistic faces. Don't draw halfway; pull the character's expressions to the very edge. Enhance the impression of the moment. Chris Hart is the best-selling author of art instruction books covering such topics as manga, cartoons, and comics, and as Chris Hart says, "Don't settle for the ordinary. By tweaking, or *pushing*, a character's facial expression, you get that extra energy and vitality that can make a memorable moment." Look at Figure 4.2 to see what I mean.

Figure 4.2
Pushing a character's expressions.

Body Language

Of course, people don't always express themselves with just their faces. Bodies can convey a lot about how people are feeling and even help them communicate. To see what I mean, take a look around you when you're in a crowded place and see what your fellow humans behave like. For example, a guy with hunched shoulders, his hands in his pockets, staring at his feet while he walks, is obviously not a happy camper. Try to notice postures and gestures and then doodle them to use in your comics later. Also, be on the lookout for interesting physical quirks or habits you can give to your imaginary characters.

As with facial expressions, you should exaggerate a character's posturing. The slumped-shouldered guy shouldn't just hunch his shoulders forward; he should be practically bowed over as if the weight of his depression is too much for him to carry. The most dramatic example of physical exaggeration you see, and what has become a staple of cartoons, is what is called the *take,* where a character over-reacts to something unexpected, as shown in Figure 4.3.

Hands

Hands, too, can convey a lot about a person. For example, people frequently use their hands to gesture when they talk. It would behoove you, then, to draw

Figure 4.3
The take.

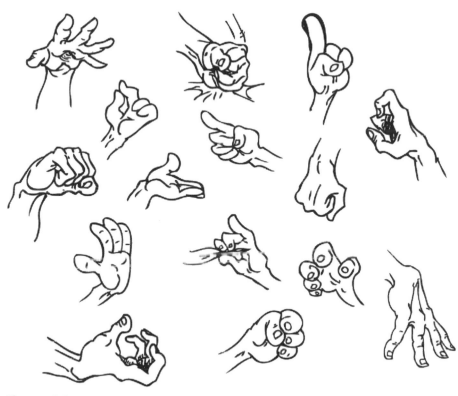

Figure 4.4
Expression can come through hand gestures.

interesting and expressive hands on your characters. Take a look at Figure 4.4 for a wide range of expressions that are visible through hands. One of the ways most artists learn to draw hand expressions is by posing and drawing their own hand (the one they're not currently drawing with, that is). You can also convince your friends to pose their hands for you, or you might take a sketchpad to a crowded mall and see how other people use their hands when conveying messages.

Expression Through Symbolism

Cartoons are an art form rich in symbolism. You need not always rely on physical gestures or facial tics to express a character's emotion; a miniature storm cloud above a guy's head could be used to demonstrate that he's angry, as could steam-geysers coming out his ears. Hearts popping out of a guy's eyes while his tongue flops out and hits the floor could represent a fellow in love. There are lots of little symbols you've probably witnessed in comics and cartoons before; the ones in

Figure 4.5
Comic-art symbols.

Figure 4.5 are just a sampling. Make it a habit to find and catalog as many as you can, because you never know when one might come in handy.

Posing Characters and Lines of Action

You must learn the physical laws of nature and what things really look like before you can stretch them out of all proportion, breaking all the rules. Just like many rock musicians learn to play their instruments before playing wild riffs on stage, a cartoonist should learn to see as an artist before doodling crazy characters. For this reason, you should make it a point to practice figure drawing and study basic human anatomy.

If you get stuck when trying to draw a character in a specific pose, try sketching a stick figure in that pose and build the model over that skeletal framework. Alternatively, ask a friend to pose for you, or use a mirror and draw yourself. What you really want to look at are proportions, and what body parts are in front of or behind other body parts when the body is in a specific pose. This process can take a while to learn, and you might want to take figure-drawing classes at an art school to get really good at it.

In cartoons, poses should not appear static. Cartoon characters are always in motion. They should appear animated even if they're not. One trick is to draw special guidelines called *lines of action* that show the general direction and flow of the cartoon character's movement. Lines of action usually follow the character's

Figure 4.6
Lines of action.

spine, but this is not always the case. Look at Figure 4.6 to see some examples of lines of action.

Caricatures

A *caricature* is a picture of someone that exaggerates his or her most striking or unusual features. You should be able to recognize the person, even if the caricature is funny, but at the same time recognize that the person does not actually look exactly like the drawing.

Drawing caricatures is a useful skill for any cartoonist. For one thing, you might end up as a lead animator for a TV program similar to *The Simpsons*, where guest stars show up almost weekly, and need to draw cartoon characters based on those real-life people. Or you might set up an easel and sell your drawings in a famous travel location, making caricatures of paying tourists. You might even decide to do political or social cartoons, which make fun of popular people on a strip-by-strip basis.

All caricature, whether of the famous or ordinary, depends a lot on identifying the subject's most pronounced features—what sets them apart from everybody else—and exaggerating only those features. With celebrities, these features are often obvious because they've been fixed in the public mind by the work of other cartoonists. When determining what features should be exaggerated, imagine you had to describe the person to someone else and think about which of his or her features you would single out.

The most important thing to remember when drawing caricature is that you are not trying to create an accurate representation of the person. You are trying to create a recognizable one. It helps to look at the person, or a photograph of him

Figure 4.7
A caricature of myself.

or her, while you are drawing. Figure 4.7 is a caricature I made of myself. You should practice caricature by making an image of yourself, too.

What About Schooling?

If you are tempted to enroll in art classes over the summer—or you want to go on to college to major in art—you will only be improving your skills. Remember, though, that such classes can be expensive, and choosing whether to attend college (and which college to attend) is a big decision—and one that should not be made lightly. School programs vary widely with respect to the quality of education and instructors. Visit with a counselor, ask for as much information as the school is willing to give, and don't be shy. It's a good idea to find out what the teacher or school is offering before you or your parents part with any cash.

The following are schools that teach comic art, cartooning, or animation:

- Academy of Art College

- Art Institute International

- Brooks College

- Collins College

- Digital Media Arts College

- Ex'pression College for Digital Arts

- IADT

- Illinois Institute of Art

- ITT Tech

- Johns Hopkins University

- Platt College

- Pratt Institute

- San Francisco State University

- Savannah College of Art and Design

- Skidmore College

- The Art Institute

- The Art Institute of California

- The Art Institute of Phoenix

- The Center for Cartoon Studies

- The Joe Kubert School of Cartoon and Graphic Art, Inc.

- University of Wisconsin–Milwaukee

- Westwood College

You can use Google or another popular search engine to find out more information about these and other schools online. If you contact a school, be sure to inquire about its animation preference—that is, whether it works with 2D animation, 3D animation, or both. Also find out exactly what kind of software applications it uses, because there are no set standards in the digital media industry.

Review

In this chapter you learned about expressing yourself to the best of your abilities using your chosen medium. You explored copying the styles of other artists, synthesizing what you practice into your own unique look, and evaluating your artwork critically. You also looked at the use of facial expression, body language, symbols, and gestures as a means of communicating in comic art. Then you looked at caricature drawing and the possibility of finding a place at an art school. The next chapter discusses the layout of a comic strip or book.

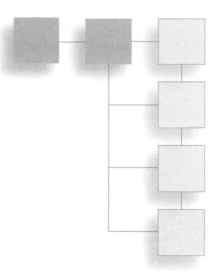

CHAPTER 5

COMICS LAYOUT AND LANGUAGE

Through repeated practice, you can become a great drawer—although it won't happen overnight, and it takes plenty of practice. You may not even be aware of it at first. A lot of techniques you learn you won't really even think about. They just sink into you, and occasionally leak out to make your work look better. They're like happy artist elves. The more you practice, the more happy elves you end up with!

This chapter looks at how the most widespread comic illustrations are created. There are many aspects to this, including layout, scripting, and refinement for publication. If you've never picked up a comic before, or never paid more than a passing look at the way these stories are told, this is the chapter you can't afford to skip.

Comic Layout

Figure 5.1 shows a basic comic layout. Comic layouts are composed of the following elements:

- **Panels.** A comic wouldn't be considered "sequential art" if it weren't for panels! A *panel* is a block of art in a comic that has a frame around it; when put together with other panels, it shows sequential action. Panels are vital to story structure because each panel should show a logical progression in your story. Panels may be of any size or shape as long as the artwork fits inside. A comic strip can have anywhere from one to nine panels, in a single or

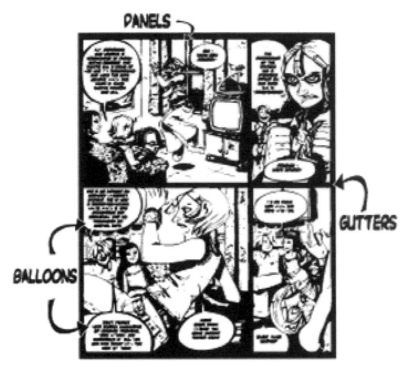

Figure 5.1
A basic comic layout. (Image courtesy Faith Erin Hicks 2005.)

double tier. A comic-book page is covered in panels—as many as will fit and still be legible. The arrangement of your panels is important. Typically, readers in the West examine comics from top to bottom and from left to right. If you leave any confusion with respect to where the reader should look next in your comic, you might lose him or her.

- **Splash panel.** Most comic books, as opposed to strips, start out with a splash panel. A *splash panel* is often a borderless panel that takes up more than 85 percent of one page's real estate. This is done on the first page of a comic, usually during the intro, and it's where readers meet the main characters (like in Figure 5.2) or get introduced to the setting.

- **Panel borders.** *Panel borders* are the borders, or frames, that go around the panels. They can make a strip look neat and tidy or free and artistic. Use a ruler and a pen with a slightly thicker tip to draw a straight-edged box around each panel. Freehand borders are finished off without a ruler, and can give your strips a sketchy effect. To keep freehand borders from going all over the place, draw the lines on with a pencil and ruler, and then draw over

Figure 5.2
A splash panel.

them with ink. Another option is to add borders in your paint editor after your drawings are scanned in as bitmap images. Use the square or rectangle tool to draw thick-stroke boxes, with the center missing out of them, and arrange them to fit over your panels. This can speed up development, but it can be more difficult if you're not used to using the software program.

- **Gutters.** The *gutters* are the white or black spaces around the page's edge and between the panels. Usually, comic panels don't butt right up against each other or bleed right off to the edge of the page. Panels share gutter margins, which operate similarly to the negative space I mentioned in Chapter 2, "Basic Drawing Techniques."

- **Titles.** The *title* is what you're going to call your comic. Coming up with a snappy title for your comic that hints at what your comic is about is important. Your comic title might appear on the cover of the book or just above and to the left of your strip.

- **Balloons.** No, I'm not talking birthday balloons. *Word balloons* help illustrate the characters' thoughts and conversations with other characters. Comic artists have to keep the number of words in each balloon relatively small.

- **Captions.** Captions help tell the story, like balloons, but they usually don't illustrate conversation. Captions are rectangular instead of round and hold only the narrator's words or descriptions of time and setting. Captions usually come in handy to establish a scene.

Comic-Strip Language

As mentioned above, you put speech and thoughts into balloons and captions in the pictures. These are often added after the drawing, in post-production. These can be different shapes, but traditionally they are round. The shape of each balloon may suggest the way something is being said.

- **Speech balloons.** The *speech balloon,* also called the *word balloon,* is the most obvious device for communication in your strips. By adjusting the shape and lettering of the balloon, you can create a wide range of personalities, moods, and emotions. Jagged lines, for instance, give the reader the impression that the character is loud or angry, while dotted lines conjure the visual that a character is quiet or whispering.

- **Thought balloons.** Often drawn as fluffy clouds with ovals for the tail, thought balloons allow the reader access to a character's private thoughts. In cinema, you might hear the main character, if he or she is the narrator of the tale, speak directly to you about his or her innermost thoughts. Thought balloons are a similar device; they are intimate and can reduce obscure questions about a character's mentality.

Speech and thought balloons do not have to be filled with text alone. Often, symbols or icons can also be used to great effect. If you haven't see one yet, usually a balloon filled with random text characters—like "$@∧#!"—can imply something far worse than if you had written it out for your readers because you allow them to fill in the blanks!

Almost without exception, these balloons are irregular in shape and are neither spherical nor rectangular. There is no rule as to whether its outline should be plain or wavy. It's simply a matter of taste. No frills should be introduced, however, as they could detract from the cartoon. The size of the balloon depends on how long the conversation in the panel is. Also, not every cartoon needs a balloon to tell a story. Indeed, some cartoonists seldom if ever use this tool. Only when the cartoonist wants to report the conversation or thoughts of the characters in the cartoon is a balloon even desirable or necessary.

Keep in mind that there should be harmony between the facial expressions in your comics and the balloon talk. When drawing the characters' facial features, it's important to consider what the speech will be, what the characters feel, and what their motivations are. Additionally, just as the face should be in harmony with the balloon talk, so too should the gestures. Otherwise, the reader will be, frankly, confused. The whole figure, from head to toe, must depict what appears in the balloons.

It is best to do the lettering before you draw the bubble outline. There are two ways to add the lettering. One is to wait until after the image has been scanned in as a raster image on your computer and then add the text using your paint editor. Another is to add the text with a fine-tip pen before scanning your image in.

If you choose the former, you can download font packages from Blambot or Comicraft. Both companies provide excellent comic fonts that look hand-drawn. These fonts work in any program you use on your computer. If you choose to go the hand-drawn way, you'll need to take a few extra steps to get the letters all the same height. First, draw parallel pencil lines and letter in between them, as in Figure 5.3. Then erase the guidelines. The letters are likely to be quite small, so it is best to use capital letters, which are clear and easy to read. If your handwriting isn't legible, find a friend whose is. If you plan for translation into foreign languages at a later date, make sure your balloons are big enough to hold your text and still have plenty of margins for resizing.

Figure 5.3
Hand-drawing a word balloon.

Figure 5.4
Examples of word balloons.

Whichever method you choose to use, keep the speech short. Otherwise, the strip gets complicated and the bubbles will take up too much room. Remember: You're not writing a book here. You're drawing a comic. Your dialog must be simple and in character at all times.

Also, make sure to allow room for the bubbles when you sketch your pictures. When positioning speech bubbles, remember that people in the West read from left to right down the frame. They will usually read the bubbles at the top before they read bubbles farther down the page. Similar to how paragraphs in a book are separated, you can also divide text in balloons in the same panel by drawing separate balloons and adding connecting tails between them. The length of the tail can indicate longer pauses in speech. Look at Figure 5.4 for some examples of speech and thought balloons.

Special Effects

Sound effects make the average strip more fun to read. As you read, you imagine the noises indicated by the effects, making the experience not unlike watching a film. You add sound effects by using words and shapes that suggest the sound. Common ones are crashes and explosions, such as POW, BOOM, and WHAM, but there are dozens of others you can imagine. Sound effects do not have bubbles around them, the way speech and thought balloons do. They can be hand-drawn, or you can type them in using a paint-editing program on your

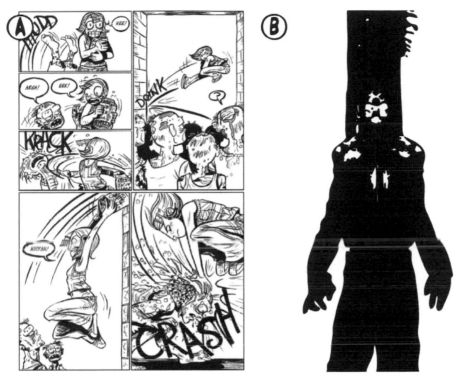

Figure 5.5
A: Whiz lines make things look like they're in motion; B: Silhouettes make images look more dramatic.

computer. They're usually in a different font, larger in size than the rest of the text, and more exaggerated.

The following are other special effects that you can use in your comics. Avoid overusing them, as continued use will decrease their effectiveness.

- Every so often, it is good to let active characters or objects overlap the panel borders, appearing to burst free from their comic prison.

- *Whiz lines* (see Figure 5.5) are kind of like the vapor trails an airplane leaves in a clear blue sky. They show where objects are in motion within a panel. Whiz lines need not be straight, but they do take a lot of practice to make them look right.

- *Silhouettes* (also shown in Figure 5.5) are a good way to add visual interest to your strips. The stark contrast of black-on-white adds drama to the action. Using different silhouettes for your pictures can also make them look creepy or mysterious.

- You can highlight the effects of a particular scene by changing the shape or look of the panel border.

- Blackouts are easy to draw—just eyes and word balloons—and let the reader fill in the details. That said, they can be overused by lazy artists and are generally not appreciated by audiences.

The Breakdown

You have to decide how to split up the sequence of your story into individual scenes and frames. This is known in the industry as the *breakdown*. The first frame of any comic is usually an establishing shot that sets the scene up. The rest of the panels initiate the action. The very last panel delivers the punch (and in the case of gag strips, the punch line).

Before putting pencil to paper, you'll have to rough out the breakdown of your strip in your head. When you do, keep in mind the relationship between the panels. The action must progress through each panel, and the way you lead the reader's eye through the panels and focus on the action as your story unfolds is through composition.

Composition

The reader's eye is drawn compulsively to the center of action in a picture. This does not happen by accident, however. Artists arrange the elements of their drawings in a particular fashion because of what "feels right." There are also several methods of composition, based on historical artistic tenets, that will help you decide how to organize the elements of each of your comics.

Shape and Scale

One of the first sets of considerations for any work of art is the size, shape, and general scale of the artwork to be presented. If you already know you're going to do a single- or double-tier comic strip, as would appear in a newspaper or comic album, or that you are doing full-page color comic pages, then you are ahead of the game. You also need to consider how much room you need to tell your idea. In a typical strip with a single tier, you may have up to five or six panels. Decide how many panels you have to work with before you start drawing; these considerations will govern the rest of your composition.

Center of Interest

The center of interest in each panel must be clearly defined so that the reader's eye will be led directly to it. This can be defined compositionally through a number of well-tried methods:

- **Compositional lines.** The reader's eye is led to the action through compositional lines and tangents, such as arms, furniture, walls, landscape features, and more. Most of these lines point to the center of interest, as you see in Figure 5.6.

- **Hiatus.** Sometimes, the center of interest is given prominence by a *hiatus*. That is, there is a clear space around the object of attention, or thicker lines are drawn around its perimeter. In this way, the object is singled out.

Figure 5.6
All the lines in the last panel point to the center of interest.

- **Contrast.** The center of interest may have a different tone or color that separates it from the rest of the panel. In a crowd of black-and-white penguins, for example, one covered in strawberry jam will pop out to the reader.

- **Viewpoint.** The perspective system you choose will have a huge impact on your picture, sometimes making innocuous pictures appear dramatic. One important choice is eye level—that is, whether you use a bird's-eye view, a mouse-eye view, or something in between). A reader's viewpoint affects how he or she interprets a scene. Imagine you're an angel with the ability to always get the best seat in the house, seeing the action from the very best angle every time, and then draw the scene from that angle.

- **Light and shadow.** As mentioned in the section "Special Effects," lights and shadows can enhance a picture. They can also lead the reader's eye through the picture.

- **Color.** Most design schools require students to study the color wheel. In the color wheel, the primary hues (red, yellow, and blue) are mixed to produce secondary colors (orange, green, and purple). When these colors are in turn mixed with the primary colors, tertiary colors are created, and so on. (Roughly 150 hues are discernible to the human eye.) The color wheel is further divided into warm and cool colors. Cool colors have less visual impact and induce a feeling of calm and space, while warm colors, like vibrant reds, can produce an excited response. By using a mixture of warm and cool colors, you can direct the reader's eye to the center of interest.

Refining Your Image

Setting a scene just right in order to progress the story involves some analytical work. You must encapsulate a lot of information for your reader on every panel you draw in order to tell your story in a limited space. These space constraints mean that any character or object you decide to include in a panel must serve a specific purpose. Indeed, every prop you include must be carefully considered as to its relevance in the composition.

If you look at the work of other cartoonists, you will notice that props can be reduced to an essential minimum; precedents have already been set that the public already accepts. For example, you can determine a character's profession and socio-economic status with just a few props or a certain costume. You can tell the reader whether it's day or night, stormy or nice, even if the strip is set indoors, through the use of windows.

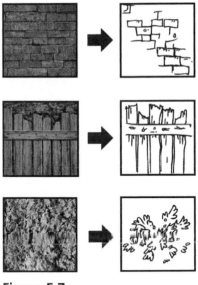

Figure 5.7
Simplify objects to speed up your work and create finer cartoon images.

Not only are objects refined to essential representations of the whole, but details and textures are too. You will notice that most cartoonists don't draw every detail in a picture; instead, they give enough to allow the reader to fill in the blanks. When a cartoonist draws a field of grass, for example, he or she seldom draws every blade of grass, but instead draws three or four blades to indicate the rest. Likewise, when drawing a brick wall, the cartoonist doesn't have to draw each and every brick; instead, he or she can draw four or five evenly spaced bricks and let the reader's imagination do the rest. Look at Figure 5.7 for some examples.

You can apply this method of visual shorthand throughout your comics. Remember: You have a limited space to convey an entire story, so the items you choose to draw must enhance rather than stray from your story. Think of it as visual real estate.

Planned Reduction

Speaking of real estate, publishers try to get the most out of their papers, meaning they often reduce the size of any printed artwork that appears in them. Indeed, if you look at most printed comics, you'll see that they are generally smaller than what one would naturally draw them. Most comic artists do not draw their cartoons at the size at which they will be printed. The size you draw your cartoons yourself is a personal matter and should be whatever you feel comfortable with.

Figure 5.8
The original image and the image shrunk for printing.

Note, however, that reducing the size a cartoon has certain effects on it. For one, reduction almost always improves the appearance of a drawing, as you see in Figure 5.8. Lines become denser and more incisive, and tiny imperfections tend to vanish. When a cartoon is reduced substantially, however, small details can seem to disappear, so bear that in mind and keep your drawings simple. The enlargement of a cartoon has almost the opposite effect to reduction: Lines become less sharp and less dense, and any imperfections are magnified. Unless absolutely unavoidable, enlargement of your work should be discouraged.

Making a Comic from Start to End

Now that the preliminary lecture is over, I bet you're ready to make some sequential art. This section shows you how to go about your work. It's not really that hard, once you develop decent work habits and a method for creation. Your only real constraint will be your imagination—and with any luck you have a large-sized imagination!

The Idea

In any cartoon, the idea is of paramount importance. It is the inventive phase of any comic. Even a crude drawing, when used to illustrate a clever idea, will get by. It goes without saying that you should steer clear of hackneyed or trite themes worn threadbare by constant use.

News editor Foster Coates used to say, "Never be satisfied with the first idea that occurs to you. Cast it aside and think of another. Then cast the second aside and the third; and keep up this process of elimination until you are sure you have the best idea possible on that particular subject." Coates theory was that the first idea you have is the idea that would naturally come to the mind of just about anybody, meaning that it will not be all that inspired. It's an idea lacking in distinction. It's obvious. The obvious idea is a hollow one, and it lacks the punch you need to get noticed. You don't want to use that. You want to find an idea that no one would pull out of a hat but you.

No one can teach you how to generate ideas that will immediately appeal to the public. That is something you must do for yourself. You must have the ability to recognize funny or remarkable incidents, and to assess how interesting they'd be if told through your artwork. The presentation of the idea is truly secondary to the conception of it.

It should come as no surprise that the most oft-heard question posed to cartoonists is, "Where do you come up with your crazy ideas?" To betray a big secret—and this you cannot tell another living soul—we do not invent a new idea every day. We don't sit around constantly doodling our hearts out, either. We all have lives. We might be inspired while at work, while in class, while taking a shower, or late at night, when we're supposed to be sleeping. Life is what inspires us. Indeed, a great portion of my cartoons have grown out of observing some funny little happening during the day and then giving it a humorous twist. Naturally, the wider your radius of observation, the better opportunity you'll have for seeing these humorous incidents. There is abundant material from which to draw all around you. Your life is surely rich in comedy as well as pathos and sympathy. The many-sidedness of life reveals an imaginative but true picture of us all, whether it's the funny things that happen in the daily grind of a coffee shop or the trials and tribulations of a kid just starting out at a new school. If you get an inkling of an idea in your mind and you roll it over in its changing phases, a number of possible ways to treat it will occur to you.

Here are some suggestions when trying to think up a decent comic idea:

- **Start with a subject.** Pick a subject you and your readers are doubtless familiar with.

- **Ask yourself if the subject is a timely one.** Some subjects are absolutely taboo during certain current events. For example, directly after the terrorist attacks on September 11, 2001, most cartoonists would not draw references to the Twin Towers or plane explosions—and for good reason!

- **Ask yourself if your idea is pertinent to everyone.** Writing a strip about how great parfait is does not work if everyone does not like parfait. The same is true of many different subjects. Gauge your target audience's preferences.

- **If you plan to print, be general rather than specific.** As long as you want your work to appear in as many publications as possible, you had better to stick to the so-called "all-in-the-family" topics.

- **Go off the beaten path.** Sometimes an ingenious little twist or clever conversation will do the job to make your comic completely novel.

Note

Regardless of what idea sparks your comic, it must show the element of humanness. Although it is true that comic characters are overdrawn and caricatured from real life, and that some may appear to be animals or robots or mythological creatures, they should not be made to do things that are too strained or inhuman. Humanness is what stories and even jokes are all about. For instance, J.K. Rowling has become a literary star due to the popularity of her British-based fantasy series *Harry Potter,* but although the pages of her books are full of the doings of wizards and witches and an occasional half-giant, the real story is about a young boy who feels small and hopeless in a big scary world—and thousands of readers can identify with him!

Here's another secret: Although a cartoonist might manage to scrape up a new cartoon, it doesn't mean that the idea behind that cartoon is a new one. If you truly examine the run of cartoons on the web, you'll see fundamental themes or ideas that are often repeated. It would come nearer the truth to tell you that a cartoon represents a new or clever interpretation of an idea. In fact, the same old comic strip may actually be repeated every three years without detection— primarily due to the shortness of the public's memory and, in some measure, the changes made in the art style, composition, or exact wording. That said, I do not advise anyone to rely on this system of repetition. The comics that really strike our fancy and leave us wanting more present seemingly fresh material on a regular basis. If you find that your ideas come sporadically (and don't worry if they do, because they do for most of us), you must learn not to depend on inspiration on a daily basis. Get yourself a sketchbook and start jotting down ideas as they come to you; then, when you're really struggling to reach your muse, just pick up your book and find one of the concepts you haven't used yet.

Scripting Your Story

Spilling your ideas onto paper and then grabbing for your pencils to draw with is often not enough. You should also write a script for your comic—and the longer your comic is, the more involved your script should be. For instance, if you're making a four-panel gag strip, you might write a short note about what it would contain and be done with it. If, however, you are writing a 15-page comic book, you need a play-by-play script. A script explains what is happening in each frame of the comic. It describes the background, what characters are present, what the characters are doing and saying, and any sound effects. Some artists choose to write their own scripts, while others illustrate scripts written by someone else. Comic scripts resemble film and TV screenplays in the way that they are written.

The first thing to do when creating a comic is to think of a plot. It needs to be funny or dramatic. The plot needs to be full of fast action to keep the reader interested. The story must progress quickly and something new must happen in each picture. The plot should follow a natural succession and have an exciting finish. Remember that the page of a comic is a fixed size, so the story needs to be divided up into the appropriate number of panel frames to fit it all in. Don't settle for the first write-through. A good script must be written, edited, re-written, and so on—until you are absolutely satisfied with the tempo, language, and other content.

Note

If you have trouble imagining what a script for cartoons should read like, visit writer Jeffrey Scott's website at http://users.adelphia.net/~getjeffrey. There you will find several sample scripts, including some he's done for *Teenage Mutant Ninja Turtles*, *Muppet Babies*, and *Dragon Tales*.

Storyboarding

Storyboards are a series of illustrations or images displayed in sequence for the purpose of pre-visualizing a motion graphic media sequence, including animations (see Figure 5.9). If you make animations, you should start by drawing a storyboard. Storyboards are loosely sketched or roughed in so the artist knows what direction to take. Don't be overly concerned with the quality of the art because, like as not, nobody is going to see it but you. Concentrate instead on determining the proper shots to help the story flow. In addition to layout and visual design, the composition of your shots can convey a lot of information about the perspective and emotion of your scene.

One important aspect of storyboarding is determining how far the camera (real or imagined) should be from a scene. In this regard, types of shots include the wide shot, the medium shot, the close-up, and variations of each.

Figure 5.9
A storyboard.

- Typically a *wide shot* is used for establishing a location or showing the relative placement of characters and objects in the scene. A wide shot is good for establishing a clear picture of where objects are located in relation to one another, but usually doesn't work well for illustrating complex emotions.

- A *medium shot* is more intimate and allows the audience to see facial expressions as well as details in props and backgrounds. A medium shot can include more than one character at a time, and can show limited action within the frame.

- The *close-up* is an emotional shot. It's very good for showing subtle shifts in facial expressions or to show important details when used as a cutaway. For example, if you want to demonstrate a bomb squad trying to diffuse a bomb, you might cut to an extreme close-up of the officer's hands working on the mechanics of the explosive. Close-ups can only show very limited action due to the limited space.

Tip

From a graphic standpoint, it's always recommended to show diagonals in your compositions. This happens naturally when you use a low- or high-angle camera for a scene, but can also be achieved by rotating the camera so that the horizon line is at a slight diagonal. When you use foreshortening, the perspective adds diagonals to the scene naturally.

Figure 5.10
Many artists use the rule of thirds. (Image courtesy Sarah Ellerton, 2007.)

Rule of Thirds

Many artists also use the rule of thirds in their compositions. The *rule of thirds* refers to the practice of dividing an image into thirds, length- and height-wise, and is widely used because it achieves a natural balance in the frame (see Figure 5.10). Placing all your characters and objects in the dead center of each frame makes for boring compositions, so try to achieve a sense of balance in each frame and find interesting ways of weighting the objects in a frame or on the intersecting lines.

Another consideration when storyboarding is to maintain the visual relationships of your scenes so readers don't get confused. For example, if you compose a scene of a couple talking to each other across a table, keep the scenes consistent. If the man is on the right and the woman is on the left in the wide shot, it should remain that way throughout the cartoon. Sometimes you'll need a character to be in a certain place for narrative considerations—stage your characters in a way that makes visual sense with the story, but doesn't block other important aspects of the scene. If several things are happening concurrently, the logistics of the scene will order character placement. If you show one character talking to another while a villain sneaks up behind him, it is essential to keep both actors in the foreground, with the reader able to see the villain sneaking up from behind. As with stage acting, you generally don't want to show characters talking for long periods or overcrowding other aspects of the scene.

Note

If you need more help with storyboards, take a look at Mark Simon's books. He's the author of *Storyboards: Motion in Art, 2nd Edition* and *Producing Independent 2D Character Animation: Making and Selling a Short Film* (both published by Focal Press). He gives helpful advice on storyboarding.

Digital Art and Color

This section demonstrates step-by-step how leading web comic creators go from hand-drawn and inked pieces of paper to fabulous digital art—as in Figure 5.11—and how they color that art using paint programs on their computers. It's not a very complicated process, but you do need to have a computer with a paint or image-editing program installed on it, as well as a

Figure 5.11
A character comes to life through digital editing.

digital scanner. A digital art tablet, like the ones available from Wacom, is optional, but preferred by many. Some schools and universities now offer such hardware on campus, and they are often available for public use.

Note

This section assumes you are drawing a full page for a comic book or graphic novel, but the same principles apply for creating a short gag strip or webtoon.

Drafting the Digital Image

First, do lots of thumbnails, sketches, and research before drawing. Of your thumbnails, choose the very best one in terms of composition and communicating your story. Draw a *rough*, or storyboard. This is important because it helps you focus on the upcoming drawing, and your results will be improved. Then start your drawing by sketching it on paper with a Col-Erase blue pencil.

Creating Sketch Lines with Your Computer

If you do not have a Col-Erase blue pencil, you can use a computer to create the sketch lines. Here's how:

1. Sketch your image lightly in pencil on paper.

2. Using your digital scanner, scan the page into a digital image on your computer.

3. Open the image in your image-editing program. (Note that in this exercise, I'm using Adobe Photoshop, because it is the standard in the industry at the time of this writing. If Photoshop is outside your price range, there's a free knock-off called Paint Dot Net available for download online.)

4. Open the Image menu, choose Adjustments, and select Hue/Saturation.

5. The Hue/Saturation dialog box opens (see Figure 5.12). Check the Colorize checkbox and drag the Hue slider until a cyan (light blue) color effect appears. (Note: If you can't see this happening onscreen, you might have to check the Preview checkbox.)

6. In the Layers palette, on the right side of the screen (see Figure 5.13), adjust the Opacity value to 45%, give or take. (Note that if the Opacity setting is grayed out, it's because the layer you're on is the background layer, which is locked by default. To fix this, right-click the name of the background layer, choose Duplicate Layer in the menu that appears, select a name for your new layer, and click OK. Then select the original background layer, select Edit > Fill, and fill the entire layer with the color white at 100%. Finally, adjust the Opacity setting on the new layer you created as outlined earlier in this step.)

7. You now have the same image you would have if you had started with a Col-Erase blue pencil; print it out on a color printer and continue with the rest of this guide.

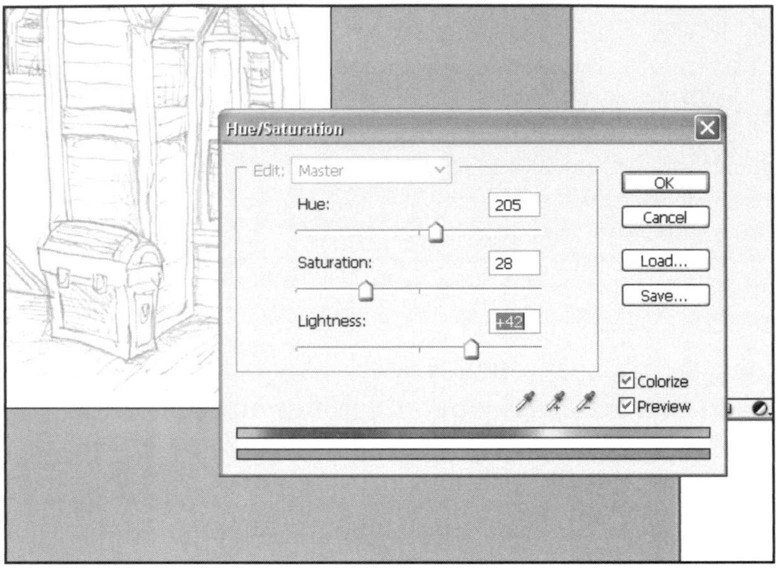

Figure 5.12
The Hue/Saturation dialog box.

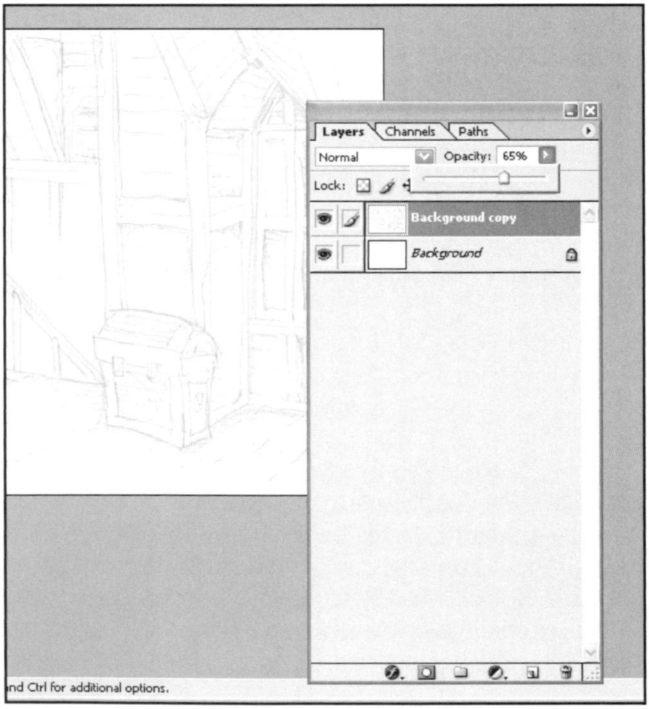

Figure 5.13
The Layers palette.

After you have your sketch lines made, do the following:

1. Go over your sketch lines with heavier black lines in the medium with which you feel most comfortable. Most comic artists use a variety of pens and ink. Don't worry about word balloons or text yet.

Tip

You can, if it feels right to you, add panel borders at this time, or you could opt to do it later on the computer using line or shape tools in your image-editing program.

2. Scan your finished image into your computer at 200dpi (dots per inch) or better to produce high-resolution line art.

3. Open your scanned image in Adobe Photoshop or whatever image-editing program you're using. (Note that these steps assume you're using Photoshop.)

4. Open the Image menu, choose Adjustments, and select Brightness & Contrast.

5. The Brightness & Contrast dialog box opens. Raise the Contrast value to +15%. This creates bolder, darker lines and makes the white of your paper color appear even whiter.

6. Optionally, raise the Brightness value.

Tip

Use the Preview option to make sure you're doing this right. You want the black lines on your image to pop out and the blue lines to recede. You also want imperfections on the paper you drew on to disappear, if possible. Whatever you do, don't sacrifice image quality; if you raise the Brightness or Contrast values too much, all the lines will start to turn grainy and eventually disappear.

7. Save your file in the native format (in my case, as a PSD file). This preserves the work you've done so far.

8. Next, create a flattened image you can mess around with outside of Photoshop. To do so, open the File menu, select Save for Web, and choose a JPEG or JPG file type at 100%. (The Save for Web dialog box has the added benefit of giving you a real-time preview of the image as it would look saved as a JPEG or JPG.)

Figure 5.14
When you zoom in to look at a raster image, it gets pixilated quickly.

Adobe Photoshop is a raster image editor. That means no matter what you do in Adobe Photoshop, your image will remain pixilated. *Pixels* are those tiny dots of color you see when you zoom way in to look at a picture (see Figure 5.14). You can choose to stay with raster images when working on your comic or to switch to vector images. Vector images are not drawn in pixel-by-pixel, but are instead mathematically generated by spline curves so they look good no matter how far you zoom in on them. I typically use vector because I prefer the crisp smooth lines vector carries, but it's really up to you.

If you choose to work with vector images, you have to switch to a vector editor at this point. A *vector editor* uses both bitmap images and vector images and can merge the two. Many artists use Adobe Streamline for vector editing, but since the release of version CS2, Adobe Illustrator, which is the companion to Adobe Photoshop and is often available in the Creative Suite bundle, has included Live Trace options that expand its vectorization versatility. I'm going to use Adobe Illustrator CS2 for this exercise.

1. Open your saved JPEG or JPG file in Adobe Illustrator. When you click the artwork, a bounding box appears to show you what you have selected.

2. Click the down arrow next to the Live Trace button and choose Comic Art from the list that appears (see Figure 5.15).

3. Your image changes on screen. If you do not like the results, open the Edit menu and choose Undo, and then try another one of the Live Trace presets.

4. When you are satisfied with the vector version of your image, click the Expand button on the main menu bar. This reduces the vector image to *paths,* which you can right-click and ungroup to work with separately.

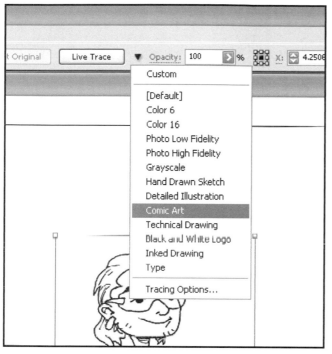

Figure 5.15
The Live Trace preset options.

At this point, you have many different choices. You could color your picture within Adobe Illustrator or you could take the image back into Adobe Photoshop and color it there. To export your image so that you can open it in Photoshop, go File on the main menu, choose Export Preview, and select the JPG format at 100% quality. Save it with a different name than what you've used before, so that you keep your original unscathed. Then open the JPG you've just exported into Photoshop. Whichever program you choose to color in, you're going to take your line art and color it next, as shown in Figure 5.16. I prefer the color options in Adobe Photoshop, so I will show you how to add color using it.

Computer Colorization

In Photoshop, your final inked image should comprise a single layer in the Layers palette. To colorize it, do the following:

1. Double-click on the layer containing the inked image and call it Lines.

2. Right-click the Lines layer and choose Duplicate Layer from the menu that appears.

Figure 5.16
Before and after colorization is done on computer.

3. Name the duplicate layer Fill.

4. Click and drag the Fill layer so that it is beneath the Lines layer in the Layers palette hierarchy.

5. Select the Lines layer, set the Blend mode to Multiply, and lock the layer by clicking the lock symbol in the Layers palette. You should now have, in order from top-down, a Lines layer, which is set at Multiply and locked, so it won't get messed up; a Fill layer; and a Background layer, which you won't see or use (see Figure 5.17).

6. With the Fill layer selected, pick colors from your Colors palette and fill in sections of your picture with the Drop Bucket tool. Be sure you fill only those areas that have closed paths; otherwise, the entire picture will get colored. (Open the Edit menu and choose Undo if you make a mistake.)

Tip

Choose a color palette that evokes the correct feeling. I typically use a separate image I have stored on my computer that I feel is very evocative, and I sample colors directly off it using the Eyedropper tool.

7. When you're ready, switch to the Brush tool and paint color in with it.

Figure 5.17
How your Layers palette should look.

Tip

> You can adjust size and type of brush in the Brush dialog box, which you access by clicking the down arrow next to the Brush type on the Options bar (see Figure 5.18). You can also find various other brush presets in the Brush dialog box by clicking the arrow button on the right of the box, like Dry Media Brushes and Faux Finish Brushes—and you can download and add more brushes from online at places like http://www.Brusheezy.com and http://www.PSBrushes.net. When doing the initial painting of comic characters, I tend to use a round brush set to 0% Hardness.

8. Most of the focal elements in your picture should have more than one color applied. For instance, if you're painting a bush, don't just use one shade of green. Use two or three shades of that hue. To make elements look even more lifelike and less cartoonish, put highlights and shadows on them. To do so, create a new layer and call it Lights.

9. Pick a white color for your brush.

10. Set the brush Opacity to 40%.

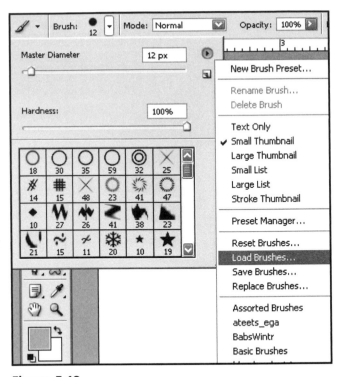

Figure 5.18
The Brush dialog box.

11. Choose an element of your picture to which you want to add highlights. Be sure you know which direction the light is coming from in your imaginary world so that you know where to place the highlights.

12. Paint a small bit of white in the spot where the highlight should go (see Figure 5.19).

Note

If you decide your highlights are too bright, you can play around with the Lights layer's settings, such as Fill or Opacity, until you get them to look just right.

13. Repeat steps 8–12 to make your shadows; just call its layer Darks and use black paint instead of white.

Figure 5.19
Paint highlights using a separate layer.

Note

Not only can you adjust these layers independently from one another, you can change their Opacity, Fill, and Blend mode on-the-fly, speeding up your color production. You can turn the visibility of separate layers on and off by toggling the eyeball icon to the left of their thumbnails.

14. Save your image as a PSD file so that you preserve the design layers for any later editing.

One last thing: Photoshop has many different selection tools, including the Magic Wand tool, which can select areas of the same color. It is particularly useful for cleaning up your Fill layer. You can also use Photoshop's Gradient Fill tool to drop color gradients in for backgrounds and objects, using the Magic Wand tool to select those areas first. This can have interesting results, as you can see in Figure 5.20.

Adding Effects

You're probably wondering about the word balloons and text. Thought we had forgotten them, didn't you? Well, these are the last pieces of a comic placed on in post-production. Most comic artists do the pencils, the inks, and the color, and another team member adds the balloon talk. But you can do all four tasks yourself.

Figure 5.20
A Gradient Fill added to the background of an image.

To add special effects, you can choose to download Comicart or Blambot's add-ons or not. There are several plug-ins available to the professional comic artist, but many of them will cost you; for now, you can do most of the work yourself for free. Draw your own speech and thought balloons and narrative caption boxes, either in your image-editing program or on paper. If you choose to draw them on paper, you're going to want to trace them over your original blue-pencil sketch so that you get the appropriate placement down pat beforehand (there are other ways to do it, but this is simplest).

Ink your balloons/boxes the same way you did your comic art, scan them in, adjust their brightness, and vectorize them if you like. When at last you put them in the same image as your layered PSD file, name their layer Balloons and drag-and-drop this Balloons layer to the top of the hierarchy in the Layers palette. The balloons will have a funny white space all around the outside of them; use the Magic Wand tool to select this empty space and press your Delete key on your keyboard to get rid of it. If your balloons or boxes are out of sync with your comic art, use the Move tool to nudge them into proper position.

Now that you have your balloons in place, you just need to type in the text. You will use the Type tool for this. The Type tool gives you all the options you need to adjust the font, size, and appearance of the text. Each block of text will appear in its own layer in the Layers palette, starting with a T thumbnail. There are several free fonts online at sites like http://www.1001freefonts.com and http://www. Urbanfonts.com that can help you truly express yourself. Choose fonts that are relatively clear and easy to read. One of my favorite fonts is Witzworx, created by Ron Evry. You can download Witzworx online at http://www.ronevry.com/ witzworx.html.

To manage and organize your text blocks, create a new layer set (click the folder icon at the bottom of the Layers palette) and call this layer set something like Balloon Talk. Drag-and-drop all the text layers into the Balloon Talk layer set and make sure that it resides above the Balloons layer in the hierarchy of the Layers palette.

Save your PSD (or other native) file and export a separate image as a JPEG/JPG for placing on the web or TIF/TIFF for printing. If you're saving something for the web, you can use Adobe's Save for the Web function to optimize the image, condensing for faster load times. If you're saving something for print, you want to make sure it's high quality and high res, often around 300dpi and 16-bit color depth. The difference between the two types of images can often be around 2MB!

Tip

If you want to see a good example of the comic-creation process by a real comic artist, go online to the home of the creator of *For Better or For Worse* at http://www.fborfw.com/features/ makingof. There you can watch as Lynn Johnston prepares her comic strips for syndication.

Review

In this chapter, you learned about the layout of comics, how the essentials like panels and balloons are used to better effect, and how to use compositional tenets to bring your comics to life. You also looked at how a comic page is prepared and colored with computers. Now you know all the fundamentals to making a comic-art page on your computer. Astound your friends and family with what you can do, because now that you know the secrets to making comic pages, you're ready to start making your own comics in earnest!

Chapter 6, "Heroic Story Writing," shows you all the details of writing comic books, graphic novels, and other hero-based tales. I'll reveal a basic formula developed by the best storytellers in our day and age. If you want to write a story involving drama and superheroes, turn to that chapter. Chapter 7, "Gag

Writing," covers the aspects of writing funnies and situational comedy. If you have any questions about writing joke strips, turn to that chapter. If you don't need storytelling tips, however, you can skip to Chapter 8, "Principles of Animation," for lessons on making animated cartoons. For instruction in putting your strips on the Internet for everyone to read, turn to Chapter 11, "Spinning a Web."

CHAPTER 6

HEROIC STORY WRITING

There are comics with as many different story styles as there are readers for them. There are superhero comics, non-superhero comics, graphic novels, and illustrated stories. In this chapter, you'll learn how to write comic books and graphic novels, regardless of type. There's a lot to writing, such as creating memorable characters and suspenseful storylines, which you'll explore here.

Note

> If you need help writing or would like more information on how to write stories, you might check with your local secondary education institution for classes or workshops—or at the public library for books on the topic.

Writing the Perfect Story

There are many exciting genres in comics: science fiction, fantasy, western, horror, fighting, superheroes, contemporary adventure, and more. Many comics straddle more than one genre simultaneously, without detriment. Think of your much-loved movie or book series, then try to figure out what genre it falls under, because odds are you will want to design comics carried out in that genre.

Once you determine the genre of comic you want to write, you're ready to put together a narrative. Writing a wonderful yarn is no small feat, but if you take the following suggestions to heart, it should be easier:

- Make up stories every day. Work on your tales "in the cracks"—that is, any time you can. I used to draw cartoons and comics while sitting in the high-school cafeteria, and no one could faze me because I was "in the zone."

- All writing must communicate ideas clearly. This is achieved through unity of purpose. Identify and remember your audience, and write on their level. Always use the right wording to convey your meaning.

- Choose your viewpoint, or who's telling the story, early on and stick with it.

- Don't ever create "stick figures" to hang your plot on. I don't mean that you can't make a comic book about stick figures, but that you should endeavor to make every character (including the setting) compelling and interesting.

- Outline your characters, settings, and plots/subplots on paper so you don't lose track of where you're headed or what's going on. Keep in mind that all events must have causes; stories are essentially cause-and-effect.

- Leave out any part the reader is likely to skip, like back stories, long descriptions, and the like.

Comic-book creators make many mistakes. They may create dull, lifeless stories that lack real oomph. They may omit important details while leaving in too many irrelevant ones. They may rely on clichés or awful stereotypes. Their characters may appear too unbelievable or unlikable. Or they may lack a sense of space or environmental background, so that the characters just seem to float around the page. Avoid all these mistakes and others.

Before devising the perfect story, ask yourself the following:

- Who are your characters?

- What setting backdrops their adventures?

- What is the premise of your story?

- And what are your characters going to do?

Comic Characters

There isn't a quick-and-dirty way to invent characters for comic books, graphic novels, and cartoons. There are, nonetheless, certain strategies that can help you lay the foundation of your character's personality, history, and motivation. Once you have this groundwork, all that's left is to draw the character; the pieces will all fit together.

Origin

As you create your character, it's important to imagine his or her origin. *Origin* refers both to the place from which your characters come and the story of how they got to be where they are today. For instance, Spider-Man, a.k.a. Peter Parker, was a mild-mannered boy reporter bitten by a radioactive or genetically altered spider. The spider's bite transformed Peter into the web-slinging superhero. Most comic-book characters have an origin steeped in fantasy, mystery, and dumb luck.

Motivation

A character's motivation can explain why a character acts or reacts a particular way, and is therefore an important part of a character's makeup. Batman (see Figure 6.1) always fascinated me because his actions were borderline crazy criminal under the veneer of practiced control. He wore a cape and hood and spent his immense fortune hunting down villains at night. All of this was because his parents were killed by a trigger-happy bad guy, and Bruce Wayne (Batman's alter ego) couldn't leave his trust in the police force. He believed vigilantism to be the answer. Give your character a very clear motivation for what he or she does.

Personality

Take a moment to consider your character's personality traits. If you limit the traits your character demonstrates on your pages, your character will come off as flat and dreary. Keep your readers on their toes, learning something new and identifiable about the character every step of the way. Your characters must sport their personalities in their expressions, actions, habits, and dialogue.

Create a diamond-in-the-rough from a stick figure. First, select four major personality traits for your character (see Figure 6.2). You can make characters that are nervous, stoic, selfless, spoiled, dignified, cocky, or lots of other adjectives. The first trait should be the character's spine; this spine is a strong central trait that is admirable and something everyone wants to have. Then develop a

Figure 6.1
Batman.

Figure 6.2
Personality traits.

supporting trait that shows some value, preference, or expressiveness that is consistent with the spine. Next choose a fatal flaw for the character. This is usually a virtue carried to an extreme or a vice; either way, this trait must still remain consistent with the spine. Lastly, think of a dark side for the character: a suppressed trait kept secret that allows for personal growth.

As an example, consider Miss Marple, the doddering old sleuth in Agatha Christie's mystery stories. The following represent Miss Marple's four major personality traits:

- **Spine: Justice.** Miss Marple is always motivated to redeem good over evil.

- **Supporting trait: Curiosity and inquisitiveness.** Miss Marple is always poking her nose into other people's business and trying to figure people out.

- **Fatal flaw: Overconfidence.** Miss Marple is so confident in her abilities she comes close to the point of recklessness, occasionally confronting bad guys without any backup.

- **Dark side: Nemesis.** Miss Marple actually confronts this in one of her adventures. She is vindictive against evildoers to the point of being ruthless.

As a character exercise, observe the personality traits of people around you, such as your family members, friends, and the people at your school. If you want, write down the traits of each person you know, using these personalities as models for your own imaginative characters. Pay singular attention to the qualities that make people—and characters—one of a kind.

According to the world's leading psychologists, human beings also have nested personalities (see Figure 6.3). At our heart is our ego, which is our core identity that must be protected at all costs. Covering our ego is our superego, which is our Jiminy Cricket, our conscience, our inner parental voice. Somewhere in there is our id, which is our childlike inner voice and sense of whimsy; when we want something, and don't get it, and want to throw a tantrum about it, that's our id talking. Last of all, there's our world mask or demeanor: the face that we show to the rest of the world. Most people have multiple world masks, one for each situation and encounter.

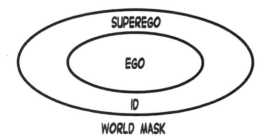

Figure 6.3
Nested personalities: ego, id, superego, and demeanor.

Spotlight on James Farr

James Farr is an artist and writer working for television and film as well as comics. He is the creator of *Xombie* (see Figure 6.4)—an online cartoon and a printed comic book series called *Xombie: Reanimated* centered on Dirge, an intelligent and friendly zombie, and his young ward Zoe, in an apocalyptic setting where ravenous zombie hordes and crazy people are the norm. Appealing to viewers of all ages, tastes, and backgrounds, *Xombie* episodes have been downloaded and viewed more than 13 million times. You can see his work at http://www.xombified.com.

Q. How old were you when you got started drawing?

A. As long as I can remember, I've been drawing, writing stories, or both. I can't really remember a time when I wasn't trying to create a character, or make one move.

Q. What inspires you?

A. Movies, music, great books. And seeing other people connect emotionally with my art.

Q. Any beginning-artist tips?

A. Always finish what you start. I think a lot of genuinely creative people have trouble finding the focus to complete a project. In other words, it's easy to get distracted, and doubly so for creative types. Half the battle is having a great idea. The other half is having the self-discipline to push it out into the world as a fully realized product. Seeing your ideas through to the end builds a great deal of focus over time, and helps save you from a house (and mind) full of abandoned ideas.

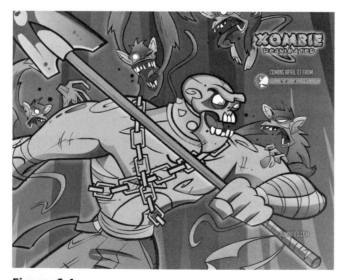

Figure 6.4
Xombie. (Image courtesy James Farr 2007.)

Q. What's the coolest thing about being a comic artist?

A. Being able to create worlds and characters that people genuinely want to visit again and again. That and getting to work from home, of course.

Q. Any other advice for young artists?

A. There is no substitute for a strong story. All the fancy explosions in the world cannot make you connect with a character, or care about an imagined event. The artwork is a method of delivery for the story, not a substitute for it. In other words, if you're going to build a house, pick a strong foundation first.

Character Profiling

Ask yourself the following questions to help establish more depth in your character:

- Where was your character born? Was he or she even born—or made?

- What was your character's family life like?

- What important events happened in your character's childhood that made your character who he or she is today?

- What are your character's special likes or dislikes? What does he or she eat, drink, and habitually do?

- Does your character have to have a secret identity? What is it?

- Does your character have a costume that hides his or her identity?

- Are there any special tools, equipment, magic items, or other props that your character uses?

- Does your character have any super powers? How did your character get his or her amazing abilities?

One option is to use yourself as the star of your own comic. You can always look to your own life as inspiration for your character. You could even write a great comic book simply about your day-to-day experiences. If you think that's too boring, add one or two small magical elements, such as an imaginary friend that comes to life or, as a premise, what you'd do if you received super powers.

In comics, you can assemble any characters you want and put them in any situation. You can create superheroes, super villains, manga boys and girls, or anthropomorphic animals, or craft stories about ordinary people. The secret is to add something of yourself to all your creations. It'll help you set your comics apart from everyone else's.

Setting

The *setting*, or background, of your comic is where your story takes place. Comics can take place anywhere and at any time, real or imagined (see Figure 6.5). Many comic books have more than one setting. Need a good setting for your story? Look around you and use the place where you live. That way, you don't have to go very far or do a lot of research to draw the scenes in your comic, because they'd practically be in your own backyard. You could also consider these great ideas:

- Where was the last place you or your family went on vacation? Can you imagine fantastic stories taking place there? Often, places people like to go to escape are just the places that make great settings in stories, because stories, after all, are a form of escape too.

- Where do you live? Can you visualize a side of your everyday world you don't normally see? What kind of characters would populate your neighborhood, and what would they do there? Neil Gaiman, the creator of the *Sandman* comics series, was inspired by the place where he lived, London.

- Imagine a place that's got everything you've ever wanted in it. What would your own version of paradise look like, and what sorts of characters would exist there?

- Now try the opposite. Envision the worst imaginable place in the universe, your own inner vision of hell. What would it look like? Why would your characters be there, and what would they do?

Don't forget time, weather, or passersby, as they are all a part of the setting. Portray all the senses: use taste, touch, sight, smell, and feeling when creating a mental picture of your setting. If you have troubles imagining the setting before

Figure 6.5
An example of a comic setting. (Image courtesy Faith Erin Hicks 2007.)

actually drawing it in your comic panels, try sketching a top-down map of the area and where everything will sit.

Premise

Most comic-book stories start with a *premise*—a short stated concept or idea. For instance, the premise of *Ranma 1/2* is that a boy gets splashed in a magic spring and is thereby cursed to turn into a girl half the time. This premise expanded into an entire series of comics and animated shows. The premise of *Pokemon* was "Gotta catch 'em all!" The premise of the early *Star Trek* show was "To boldly go where no man has gone before...." The premise, called the *high concept* by screenwriters in Hollywood, sums up the concept of the story and becomes a good catchphrase when proposing it to other people.

Plot

The sequence of events in any story is called its *plot*. In a dramatic tradition that begins with the Greek theatre, plot is broken down into three acts: a beginning, a middle, and an end. Elmer Rice, talking about this Greek drama format, said that Act I is all about getting a man up a tree; Act II is about throwing stones at him; and Act III is about getting him back out of the tree. You won't want to throw stones at anybody, but you will want to plot out your story better.

Legendary Formula

Have you ever wondered what made *Star Wars, Indiana Jones, The Matrix,* and other great films so spectacular, so immediate, and so emotionally immersive? It's because they use a universal pattern found in many narratives from around the world, including folk tales and legends. This universal pattern, called the *monomyth,* was discussed by Joseph Campbell in his book *The Hero with a Thousand Faces* (published in 1949). George Lucas has acknowledged Joseph Campbell as his inspiration when writing the screenplay of *Star Wars.*

Campbell's insight was that stories that have endured for thousands of years all share the same formula. This formula consists of a number of story stages, including the following:

- A call to adventure, where the hero is asked to start on his journey.

- A refusal of the call, where the hero declines the task until the stakes are higher.

- A series of trials, which help shape the hero by successes and failures.

- Receiving a boon, where the hero comes away with an important bit of knowledge or a special weapon.

- Final trial, where the hero faces a make-or-break challenge.

- Return to the ordinary, where the hero recovers and faces denouement, in which he applies what he's gained to improve the world.

Campbell's monomyth has influenced many artists, musicians, poets, film-makers, and game designers, including Mickey Hart, Bob Weir, and Jerry Garcia of the band Grateful Dead, who agreed to participate in a seminar with him in 1986. Film producer and writer Christopher Vogler wrote *The Writer's Journey: Mythic Structure for Writers,* in which he discusses how screenwriters can use Campbell's monomyth to make better stories. Find ways of taking this classic formula from myths and fairy tales and applying them to your writing. You'll discover that your readers will identify more strongly with the heroes and your writing will have more staying power.

Suspense

The essence of strong stories is emotional reactions within the audience. Suspense is one of the better emotional tags to pull, because suspense calls for a deep emotional response in the reader. Use characters the reader will care about and worry over. Then add conflict.

The Wee Gods of Storytelling say, "Thou shalt have conflict on every page!" Conflict breeds suspense. Conflict can be internal (within the character's own heart, often focusing on doubts or misgivings) or external (with other characters or situations). The story then becomes a question of, "Will the character overcome the conflict?" Don't answer the question too soon, however. Just when the question seems like it's about to be answered, throw in another complication for the hero.

Complications add stumbling blocks and obstacles for the hero to overcome. These complications must arise out of the story, make some real sense, and be significantly challenging without appearing hopeless. Is your story slowing down? Are things becoming too complacent? Invent a new crisis or bring an old one back. Allow the hero several failed attempts before overcoming complications; this builds suspense and reader identification.

Back Story

Back story is everything that comes before the very first panel of your comic. You should write down some back story, like the origins of your character, but you shouldn't depict it in your ongoing narrative. Why? Because most back story is dull to readers, and it is usually inconsequential. Some writers try to tell back story in flashbacks—scenes where the current narrative is put "on hold" while the writer jumps back to earlier events—in the effort of adding exposition. But flashbacks are almost as dreary as back story, so limit their use. The real purpose of a back story is to flesh out your characters and clarify their motivations and why they act the way they do (refer to the section "Origin" earlier in this chapter).

Story Starters

How do you start a story? You don't have to start at the beginning, go on until you reach the end, and then stop. Start *in medias res*—that is, in the thick of it. Strike when the iron's hot. Begin at one of the most exciting parts, and build the remainder of your tale around your nucleus ideas. You want to hook your readers on the front page so they'll continue to read your work!

Typically, come up with five or six different starting places—places where you know you could start your comic book. Evaluate each of them critically to see which would be the most engaging and eventful point of the story. If there isn't action in that very first scene, it is going to be harder to snare your reader! Choose the very best intro and draw it. Sometimes a dull intro can be spectacular if it's drawn a certain way to make it seem more dramatic than it really is, as in Figure 6.6. Show your finished intro to some of your friends and gauge their reaction.

Cliffhangers

Are you writing a continuing story that'll be told over several episodes? If so, you might want to add cliffhangers to keep your readers coming back for more. Cliffhangers, when not overused, are a great way to build suspense. The following are great examples of cliffhangers, although many of them have been used before:

- Have the story end just as a new plot twist occurs, such as Billy finding out that his companion Wanda is really a boy in disguise—and not only that, but he's Billy's long-lost twin brother!

- Have the story end just as danger looms. I can remember one of the earliest Indiana Jones comics ended with Indy in Mexico, facing an enraged bull in one of the bullfight pens. It ended right before the horns hit him, making you wonder if he'd be hurt or not.

- End on a total shocker. For instance, Phil walks from the museum to find that he's entered a parallel dimension and he doesn't know what's going on.

Figure 6.6
A dramatic depiction of an otherwise slow beginning.

Other Narrative Devices

There are several other narrative devices as old as storytelling and still used in almost every medium today. Use them sparingly. They are as follows:

- **Accordian time.** Expanding and contracting fictional time spans.

- **Advertising the future.** Explicit foretelling of upcoming events, like the ever-popular "Fasten your seat belts, folks. It's going to be a bumpy ride!"

- **Crucible.** Forcing characters that don't get along into cohabitation.

- **Dramatic irony.** Where we know something the characters don't.

- **Foreshadowing.** Subtle insinuations of what's to come.

- **Exploitation of emotions.** Playing upon the reader's hopes and fears to increase tension.

- **Planting seeds.** Seemingly unimportant clues that pay off big later.

- **Propelling transitions.** Each time one problem is solved, it causes more.

- **Plot twists.** Unexpected turns in the storyline.

- **Rerun.** Repeated events from different perspectives to emphasize a moment.

- **Time bombs.** A ticking time bomb that focuses on resolution before a catastrophe.

Review

After finishing this chapter, you should know how to compose a story, from the original premise to the dramatic ending, including how to make your characters more compelling, how to use your imagination when developing setting, and how to use the legendary formula to make your archetypal plots more powerful. You are ready to start writing! Keep a notebook or journal with story ideas in it. Whenever your imagination sparks, get up and immediately write your inspirations down before you forget them.

If you want to write joke strips and need to improve your humor skills set, read the next chapter. If not, jump to Chapter 8, "Principles of Animation," for lessons in cartooning, or Chapter 11, "Spinning a Web," for lessons in putting your work on the World Wide Web.

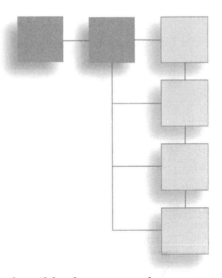

CHAPTER 7

GAG WRITING

> Children just naturally draw wacky and wild characters; however, maintaining this sense of whimsy into adulthood is frequently best left to professional idiots (er, cartoonists).
>
> —Gary Leib

Some people believe that drawing is a unique talent, given only to the lucky few, that can't be learned. Likewise, there are those who believe humor is fickle—that joke writing is impossible if a person's not a born comedian. Let me tell you: I've met several of the best gag strip artists, and they can appear meek, quiet, and demure, the same as anybody. They aren't always clowning around—but they've learned how to draw a great gag strip. (*Gag strips* are comics that set up a scene in the first panel and deliver a punchline in the last panel. The most famous gag strips are those comics that have graced syndicated funny papers for years, including *Beetle Bailey, The Wizard of Id*, and *Garfield*.)

As difficult as it is for an artist to stare at a blank page, speculating about what to fill it in with, the cartoonist's quandary is even harder. That is, the cartoonist looks at the blank page and knows that not only does he or she need to determine what to draw on it, but he or she has to convey a joke in pictures and words. This added task can break the spirit, quickly causing gag-strip artist's block. Thankfully, there are lots of hilarious situations and anecdotes that you can borrow from to make your job easier.

What's So Funny?

Nobody laughs at the same jokes. This is decidedly true. You must recognize that just as there are many different styles of drawing, there are also many styles of humor. Some of them may appeal to you more than others. Some joke strips may have you rolling on the floor, while your friends and family scratch their heads, trying to get what's so funny.

Pick a few cartoons that you know make you laugh. Then try to work out what makes them seem so funny. Is it because they have a weird twist at the end you didn't expect? Is it because they exaggerate somebody or some event from real life? Does something disastrous or embarrassing happen to someone in the strip that makes you laugh because you're glad it's them and not you?

Well-Used Comical Themes

Most humor breaks down into several comical themes, which you see used over and over again. The following are just a few examples of well-used comical themes, any one of which can make for an entire comic strip.

Escher Effect

Whenever something happens that you didn't expect—think the pie in the face that comes from out of nowhere—it's funny. As a classic example, consider Warner Brothers' Wile E. Coyote in any number of *Looney Tunes* episodes. While chasing the ever-escaping Roadrunner, the cunning and adorable scoundrel Wile E. Coyote runs off a cliff. You expect him to fall, but first he stops running, looks down, realizes his plight, stares at the camera a second, and even holds up a letter sign he pulls from his hidden back pocket. After the cartoonist gives the viewer a moment to read that the sign says ''Oops!'' gravity takes over and the poor guy falls to the canyon floor far below (see Figure 7.1). He doesn't go splat and die, however; instead, he makes a coyote-shaped hole in the ground—but then crawls back out, alive.

We not only delight in his pain, we also giggle over the unexpected humor in the situation. The laws of physics are clearly defied in order to gag us. This is known as the *Escher effect*, a special effect in cartoons in which the natural order of life is not adhered to—as long as the results are funny!

Take a look at *Scooby Doo.* In each episode, Scooby, and sometimes Shaggy, too, break the laws of physics by leaping too high, escaping from certain death,

Figure 7.1
A scoundrel takes another fall.

and eating enough food to kill a horse while staying perpetually skinny. When characters try a little Escher trick like this and twist the rules of reality, it's funny.

Schadenfreude Effect

When pain happens to you, it's not funny at all. But if the pain were to happen to someone else, and there were no social repercussions from laughing at it, you'd laugh. Look at a common cartoon episode, where the cat tries to catch a clever little mouse as seen in Figure 7.2. Just when he thinks he's caught the mouse and bites down on "him," he realizes that mouse has switched places with the feline's tail—causing the cat to howl in pain! Most cartoons wouldn't be as amusing if all the daring pain-filled antics were taken out of them. However, the violence doesn't last long, and nobody actually dies, because, as in the Escher effect, cartoon characters get back up afterward, defying all logic.

Violence without consequence is pure comic genius, and it's called the *schadenfreude effect*, borrowing a word from the Germans that means "taking pleasure from someone else's misfortune." Experiences that are normally stressful, unpleasant, or even tragic can be treated with a grain of laughter in cartoons.

Figure 7.2
The cat tries—unsuccessfully—to catch the mouse.

Doolittle Effect

Remember Doctor Doolittle, who could talk to animals and they would talk back? I don't know why, but there's something really funny about making animals walk on two legs, talk like people, and behave in a similar manner to us ungainly bipeds. This anthropomorphizing of animals is known as the *Doolittle effect*, but it doesn't just apply to animals. You can also personify objects, as long as you keep the basic look of them realistic. Imagine what one trash can might say to another: "I think I've got something between my teeth."

Animal characters that dress, talk, and walk like us are fun to draw and come with a slew of facial and body elements that work really well when drawing expressions, including whiskers, tails, hair, scales, feathers, beaks, muzzles, snouts, claws, talons, and more. Study the animal you'd like to draw before putting it in a t-shirt or jacket, and then do some more sketches of it in anthropomorphized poses. Make your animals look expressive without being too human. You want to capture the essence of intelligence without supplanting the animal's nature. For an example, look at the comic *Faux Pas* as seen in Figure 7.3.

Screen Actors Guild Effect

Acting isn't relegated to Hollywood types with nice outfits and snazzy smiles. Your comic characters are essentially actors, and sometimes the way they act is flat-out

Figure 7.3
The OzFoxes: *Faux Pas*. (Image courtesy Robert and Margaret Carspecken 2007.)

hilarious! First of all, people who act in character can appear really funny, especially when they do so at inopportune times or when situations call for other types of action. Think of a spaceship hurtling closer and closer to the sun, with no way for the ship's crew to pull out of the nosedive. If the space-cowboy pilot were to smile his usual smile and slip on his sunshades, *that* would be funny!

Characters can also act out of character for humorous effect. An especially well-known character that does this is always good for a laugh. For instance, what if the monosyllabic Tarzan of the Apes decided to become a chronicler for the *Jungle Gazette*? Or if Captain Hook in *Peter Pan* became a corporate financial advisor?

Overacting can be very funny, too. Jim Carrey, who has done some really funny movies, including *The Mask* and *Ace Ventura: When Nature Calls* (see Figure 7.4), is well known for his comic genius at overacting. He exaggerates the emotions he portrays in front of the camera and goes over the top whenever he does anything, behaving like a human cartoon. Look at some of the classic cartoons: Whenever the wolf sees a pretty girl at a nightclub, he not only acts lusty, but steam comes out his ears, his jaw drops to the floor, his tongue unfolds to hit the carpet, and his eyes roll back in his head and come out of his mouth. He then beats his fists on the table and yowls. When Porky Pig comes face to face with a ghost in a haunted house, his eyes bug out before he physically flies out of his pants and smashes out the window to get away. Overreactions are funny—especially when they come from a particular situation we've experienced before or can just imagine how we would react.

What is just as funny, and a mainstay in comedy, is the *straight man* (as seen in Figure 7.5). If you have a lunatic in your strip, you must include a straight man.

Figure 7.4
Jim Carrey as Ace Ventura.

Figure 7.5
Every clown needs a great straight man.

Being serious is also a vital part of being frivolous. Seriousness and frivolity are akin to good and evil, yin and yang. Graham Chapman plays the best deadpan roles in the Monty Python bunch, including the completely serious King Arthur in *Monty Python and the Holy Grail*. Likewise, Marge Simpson always sees the saner side of things, as opposed to her hubby Homer in *The Simpsons*.

Characters acting in character, characters acting out of character, characters overacting or overreacting, and using a straight man are all ways that you can use the *Screen Actors Guild effect* to your best advantage, thereby making your strips more entertaining.

Building Off These Themes

If you look hard enough, you'll find comic strips that demonstrate these effects and more. You can identify lots of recurring themes in the funnies, which you can then use in your own comic strips. Just as you can learn to draw from copying another artist's work, you can develop a sense of humor by doing jokes just like your favorite gag-strip artist. We all stand on the shoulders of other great cartoonists!

Once you think you "get it"—what makes comics funny—try to think of cartoon ideas of your own that would work in the same way. Don't keep copying existing comic strips; instead, use their patterns or rhythms as an inspiration to get your own funny bone going. And remember not to stray too far afield into utter nonsense; because often enough the truth is funnier than nonsense. The funniest jokes are those closest to the truth, if merely a biting truth.

Be Unpredictable

Consistency is the last refuge of the unimaginative.

—Oscar Wilde

Have you ever noticed that when a novice comedian gets up to tell a joke, he starts to sweat, his eyes bulge out of his head, and he wrings his hands or grips the microphone with white knuckles? The audience can't appreciate the comedian's joke because the comedian's nerves get in the way. The same is true of a cartoonist. If you actively think, "I've got to draw a joke, I've got to do it now," you won't get anywhere very fast, and your artwork will look forced.

It sounds like conflicting advice, but the best way to write a joke is to *not* write a joke. Instead, think of some element that you're drawing. Focus on the characters' faces or the particular way a prop will look. Let the humor come along naturally. It's there, under the surface, if you'll relax and let it leak out of your pen onto the paper.

Plus, if you can mislead your audience one way and then completely surprise it by going in another, you are sure to craft wit. Take Groucho Marx, of that crazy black-and-white trio of jokesters, the Marx Brothers. Groucho could sling some witty sayings by using this technique of misdirection. One of his often-repeated jokes goes, "Outside of a dog, a book is man's best friend. Inside of a dog, it's too dark to read." If your readers see where you're going with your comedy, then it won't be nearly as funny. But if they don't see what's coming, ending up in a completely different place, it's hilarious!

A Few Things to Watch Out For

Before you rush off to start your own gag strips, dribbling your ink all over the place and making a mess, there are some things that you should watch out for. These are pitfalls that can ruin a would-be comic genius—and if you aren't careful, they can even make you enemies.

What About #@%&*!?

Being crass or tasteless will not make your jokes funny. There's absolutely no good reason to cuss like a sailor or make unsavory references throughout your cartoons. In fact, it's a good way to turn off a large portion of your audience, not to mention validate any syndicate for turning you down. Only in very few, very rare situations does scatological, or "toilet," humor make a cartoon funny (see Figure 7.6)—and even then it's usually funny only because of the temporary shock value and wears off after a while.

For instance, *South Park* has become a cultural icon because of its crassness, but it's the fact that the characters are little kids that look like they were drawn by

Figure 7.6
Bathroom humor can be used moderately for a good laugh.

little kids, and that the bathroom humor is so outrageous, that the comedy gets laughs. The same is true of Foamy the Squirrel, the main character at Ill Will Press's *Neurotically Yours*. He's kind of like a bad-day version of The Chipmunks: a high-pitched-voiced cute mammal with an incredible mouth on him.

Just because you find the thought of farting or puking hilarious doesn't mean others will, so make something funny that's original—or at least written in an original manner. And don't rely on shock factor as a crutch.

Use of In Jokes

Just because your comic strip's funny to you and a few of your friends doesn't mean the whole world will laugh with you. Most in jokes are just that: meant to be shared by a few select people, an in crowd, and are based on "had to be there" moments. Many of them rely on several personal experiences that you would have to have shared to understand exactly what is so funny. They are hard to explain to outsiders and fail completely to be comical on a stand-alone basis.

Personal Bias or Sarcasm

While sharing your point of view about certain topics is acceptable, especially through the use of satire or sarcasm, often exposing a personal bias is not. Not everyone on the planet will agree with your bias, for one thing, and for another, it makes you come off as a pretentious person. Blunt and relatively humorless sarcasm can come across to others as resentful or bitter, if done wrong, because sarcasm is pretty difficult to read on the printed page. Look at Jim Davis' *Garfield* strips for good examples of using sarcasm. Garfield the Cat is sassy and sarcastic and always ready to share his opinions, but he does so with a true flair that makes thousands of people around the world root for him. For another good example of using sarcasm for winning responses, look at Jason Yungbluth's comic in Figure 7.7.

Creating Visual Humor

If you have a talent for visual humor—that is, telling jokes in pictures without words (see Figure 7.8)—you will have a hidden ace up your sleeve when it comes to drawing funnies. Two of the greatest comic artists at this were Gary Larson, creator of *The Far Side*, and Charles Addams, frequently featured in *The New Yorker*. Both could tell knee-slapping stories just with their drawings alone.

Figure 7.7
July 17th episode of *Deep Fried Weekly*. (Image courtesy Jason "Hot Lips" Yungbluth, 2006.)

That said, most of the time you will be making cartoons—that is, images and text that tell a joke—so never forget that there must be a proper balance between the two. If you come up with a great joke and draw two heads telling it on a page, nobody will be pleased. You have to make your art add to and illustrate your joke. The rich interplay of clever visuals and laughable words will make your cartoons a hit.

Figure 7.8
Telling jokes without words.

Review

In this chapter, you learned what makes jokes in gag strips funny and how to make ha-has for yourself. You learned the main themes that run through all situational comedies, how to incorporate them in your work, some tidbits of wisdom about making funny cartoons, and what specifically to avoid. You are now ready to start drawing joke strips; if you want to learn about animating your artwork, go to Chapter 8, "Principles of Animation." If you'd prefer to put your drawings on the World Wide Web, then flip to Chapter 11, "Spinning a Web."

CHAPTER 8

Principles of Animation

Have you ever wondered where animation came from, and what elements make up the major differences between cartoon animation and motion pictures? And here's another question: Why create animations at all? Why not stick to humdrum still figures?

The reason should be obvious. Animations simulate real action, with the still images drawn on paper leaping through time into vivid motion, as if they've come to life. There's nothing more satisfying to a cartoonist than seeing your artwork go from a flat series of images to a walking and, in some cases, even talking, character. This is why cartoonists do it. It's the spark of real creation.

Early Cartoon Making

The Persistence of Vision theory states that people compile flashes of images in time to create seamless perception in order to survive. This theory was beautifully illustrated by a clever optical contraption called a *thaumatrope* (see Figure 8.1)— a disc, held between two pieces of string or mounted on the end of a pencil that could be quickly twirled, making both sides of the disc blur together until they looked like a faultless scene. Similar to this was a novelty called the *flipper book,* or *flipbook,* which appeared worldwide in 1868. If you held the flipbook in one hand and used the other hand to flip the pages of the book, the drawings on the pages would create the illusion of continuous action.

Figure 8.1
One example of a thaumatrope.

Creating a Flipbook

Perhaps the best way for you to explore the basics of animation is for you to create a flipbook. Anyone can make a small flipbook; it's not that hard. You probably made something similar in grade school. Here's how:

1. Begin with a blank notebook containing unlined paper. Close the notebook and, using a Sharpie, draw one or more black marks across the tops of all the pages in the book. These will be your placement guidelines.

2. Open the notebook and, on the first page, draw the picture you want to start with.

3. Tear out the picture you drew and trace it on the next page, using the marks you made along the top of the notebook to line up the pages.

4. Trace the original picture on the next page, this time making subtle changes to it.

5. Repeat step 4, drawing page after page but adding subtle changes to each image, until you get to the end of your short animation.

Not sure what to draw? You might start with a guy jumping on a trampoline. The ground and the trampoline won't go anywhere, but the guy will go up and down. If you feel really inventive, you might have the guy do a somersault on the trampoline. To test your animation, flip the pages quickly by holding the flipbook in one hand and flicking the pages with the thumb of your other hand. You should see your animation come to life!

In 1896, New York newspaper cartoonist James Stuart Blackton interviewed inventor Thomas Edison. The inventor of the light bulb, Edison was then busy experimenting with motion pictures. During the interview, Blackton did some quick sketches of Edison; Edison was so impressed by Blackton's speed and skill that he asked Blackton to do a series of them, which Edison photographed. In 1906, Edison and Blackton released *Humorous Phases of Funny Faces,* a short animated picture that used about 3,000 "flickering drawings." The first of its kind, this picture was the forerunner of today's cartoons.

Windsor McCay, the creator of the popular comic strip *Little Nemo in Slumberland,* subsequently played a crucial role in the development of cartoon animation into the prodigious art form that it is today. In 1911, McCay made his character Little Nemo move, and in 1914 he stood before a projection screen as a giant cartoon dinosaur, named Gertie, moved, appearing to eat from McCay's own hand!

Among the first-ever beloved cartoon characters was Felix the Cat, a simple black-and-white cartoon character who, in the 1920s, became nearly as popular as the irrepressible Charlie Chaplin. In 1928 Mickey Mouse superseded Felix in popularity as the first-ever animated cartoon to incorporate moving drawings and synchronized sound in *Steamboat Willie,* made by Walt Disney. Disney (see Figure 8.2) astounded the world six years later when, in 1934, his company released the first full-length feature film involving drama, comedy, and professional voice talents—an 83-minute-long masterpiece called *Snow White and the Seven Dwarfs.* Nobody at the time could believe it; Disney animator Ward Kimball once recalled, "You can have no idea of the impact that having these

Figure 8.2
Walt Disney.

drawings suddenly speak and make noises had on audiences at that time. People went crazy over it." The critical and financial success of *Snow White* launched the Golden Age of animation, during which Disney's company produced the movies for which it is known even today, like *Pinocchio, Dumbo, Bambi,* and *Fantasia.* Indeed, some 80 years after the release of *Steamboat Willie,* Disney remains the most famous cartoon filmmaker in the world.

Note

Disney, known for experimenting until he found the right techniques to animate his cartoons, is credited for the standard 12 frames per second (fps) rate used in pictures today. When *Snow White and the Seven Dwarfs* came out, critics warned that the moving pictures would cause optic nerve damage, seizures, and other maladies; in response, Walt Disney hired a professional optician to consult the matter. The medical specialist determined that viewing the animations would not result in eye damage. And although animation was then filmed at 24 frames per second, the specialist determined that the human eye could detect only about half of them, prompting Disney to conduct a quick study on the veracity of filming at 12 fps. The results: Removing half the frames in *Snow White* resulted in no discernible loss of quality. Future animations could be filmed with half the labor of their predecessors! This is one of the reasons why Adobe Flash and many other animation programs default to a frame speed of 12 fps.

Although equipment and materials have improved in the intervening years, the way animated cartoons are made has changed very little. Over the next pages you will find out how cartoons—and especially webtoons—are made.

How Did They Do That?

A motion picture is a sequence of tiny pictures, or *frames.* You make a film by taking photos of thousands of segments of action. These photos are combined into one long filmstrip, with each photo comprising a single frame. A projector shines light through each frame as the filmstrip rolls through, magnifying the image on each frame onto a screen. Each frame is held still in front of the light just long enough for you to see it; then a shutter comes down while the next frame is positioned; there are typically 24 to 30 frames for each second of film, with the average of frames per second (fps) for television being 27. Although, as mentioned, the perceptual difference between 12 and 24 fps is negligible, most media producers believe that higher frame rates result in more fluid viewing and there are industry standards to keep up with. The frame rate change happens so quickly, you don't notice individual frames or the shutter. (Indeed, without the shutter between frames, the film would look like one long blur.) The afore-mentioned persistence of vision enables us to see continuous movement where there are actually multiple still images. Although digital filmmaking has since replaced the need for filmstrips and shutters with computer technology, thousands of individual frames still show action—but the speed and order in which they are shown are controlled by computer programs.

In the past, cartoon animators animated their films as follows:

1. The cartoon animator broke each scene down into different movements.

2. Each animator worked on drawing one movement at a time. Each picture drawn was called an *extreme,* and each extreme was numbered; the numbers indicated how many other stages needed to be drawn in between to complete the action. The animator had a chart representing what would happen during each split second of film, including sound effects and voiceovers; the movements drawn had to match up to the recorded sound.

3. Once all the extremes were drawn, they were passed off to other members of the animating team. These members were called *in-betweeners,* and they did all the drawings in between the extremes. The numbers on the extremes showed the in-betweener how many pictures were needed. Animators—especially in-betweeners—worked on a flat box with a glass surface called a *light box* to draw the frames of animation (see Figure 8.3); light shining up through the glass surface of the light box allowed the artist to stack several sheets of paper on top of each other and still see the papers underneath. (This is an efficient way to trace over characters to make small changes to demonstrate motion, and is still used today. It works more efficiently than simply tracing images to make flipbooks.)

4. The finished drawings were traced onto transparent sheets called *cels.* Each cel was turned over and painted on the back, so that brush strokes were not apparent from the front.

5. The cels, when dried, went to shooting, where they were photographed. The type of camera used to photograph cartoons was a special cartoon camera, which could take stop-motion pictures and combine them all into one reel of film. Background scenery was painted on long rolls of paper and laid on the plate of the cartoon camera with the cels placed on top of it. The background scenery could be rolled to either side; as the camera took pictures, this made it look as if the character was moving across the background. (This is why, if you're paying careful attention to some old *Scooby*

Figure 8.3
Students using electric light boxes in Prof. Brian A. Barsky's "Art of Animation" course at the University of California, Berkeley. (Image courtesy Brian A. Barsky, 2002.)

Doo Where Are You? episodes, you'll see items in the background that are about to move painted a slightly different shade; they were actually on different cels!)

If this sounds tedious, it is. Indeed, if you had watched a studio work to produce a single cartoon before the advent computers, you would have been mind-boggled. To get from hand drawings, like in Figure 8.4, to animated images was a long process that often involved several people and years of work.

How They Do It Today

Two-dimensional animation principles have changed little over the years, but today it is often done on—or assisted by—computers, making the need for cel painting and special cameras obsolete. Instead, figures are created and/or edited digitally using bitmap or vector graphics (see Figure 8.5). This animation approach involves automated computerized versions of such traditional animation techniques as in-betweening (now called *tweening*), morphing, onion-skinning, and rotoscoping. There are even some popular cartoons regularly created on computers that never leave the digital environment; these shows are

Figure 8.4
All cartoons start with drawings of characters—and end with them leaping off the pages.

Figure 8.5
Animation goes digital.

produced by skilled animators and include such programs as *Foster's Home for Imaginary Friends*, *The Powerpuff Girls*, *The Grim Adventures of Billy & Mandy*, and *El Tigre: The Adventures of Manny Rivera*.

There are several popular 2D animation software applications, including Adobe Flash, Mirage Studio, Toon Boom Studio, Anime Studio, and DigiCel Flipbook. Pricing for these is listed in Chapter 1, "So You Want to Be a Comic Artist. . . ." Most of these products can output files for the web, TV, or video with ease—and many of them have a similar look and feel. It goes without saying that you should find the application that suits you best before you make any purchasing decisions.

Adobe Flash

You are probably most familiar with Adobe Flash, previously Macromedia Flash, because of the many Flash animations you see on the web. A Flash animation, or webtoon, is an animated film created using Adobe Flash animation software and distributed in the SWF file format. Webtoons can be created in Flash or with other programs capable of writing SWF files.

In the late 1990s, most Internet users were stuck at a bandwidth of about 56 kilobytes per second (Kbps). Many animators employed Flash to create projects intended for Internet distribution because Flash allowed artists to release cartoons and interactive experiences that were well under 1MB in size. Moreover, Flash could stream audio and high-end animation.

In 1999, the first noted use of Flash was by *Ren & Stimpy's* creator John Kricfalusi, when he set out to bring cartoons to the World Wide Web. Soon after, webtoons began popping up everywhere. Some became so trendy—due to programming networks such as MTV or G4—that they appeared on national TV, like *Happy Tree Friends* and the politically minded *JibJab* shorts. Some, like James Farr's *Xombie* (see Figure 8.6), became DVD productions with popular comic merchandise and toy lines.

Although Flash may be capable of integrating bitmaps as well as video, most Flash toons are created using vector-based art, which often results in a cleaner graphic appearance. Some of the symptoms of badly made Flash animations include jerky movements, interpolated character movements, and abrupt changes from front to profile views. To find out more about Adobe Flash, visit http://www.adobe.com/products/flash.

Figure 8.6
Xombie. (Image courtesy James Farr, 2007.)

Bauhaus Mirage Studio

Mirage's primary mission is to create a truly paperless system of animation. That means you never have to draw on paper to come up with complete cartoons! This is very helpful for animators using digital drawing pen tablets like the ones manufactured by Wacom. Mirage (seen in Figure 8.7) can work in conjunction with Flash or by itself, and comes with tools that enable you to replicate every traditional 2D animation technique, including cel painting, collage/cut-out animation, rotoscoping, stop-motion animation, crayon drawing, motion graphics effects, integrated video, and more. Mirage even has a digital light table, which enables you to create in-betweens. And due to the wonders of Mirage's real-time rendering engine, most of the layers created in Mirage look just like they would if you'd created the artwork on paper. To see more of Mirage Studio's features and demo reels made with it, visit http://www.bauhaussoftware.com.

Toon Boom Studio

Winner of the Primetime Emmy Engineering Award, Toon Boom Studio is a sleeker package than Adobe Flash 8. Made by animators for animators, Toon Boom Studio (see Figure 8.8) features a full-screen rotary drawing table with onion-skinning, an exposure sheet, and a virtual light table for in-betweening. It works fluidly with pen tablets so you never have to use paper in your designs if you don't want to. Toon Boom Studio's most important feature is its peg-based motion-path system and its virtual 3D environment. You can create seemingly

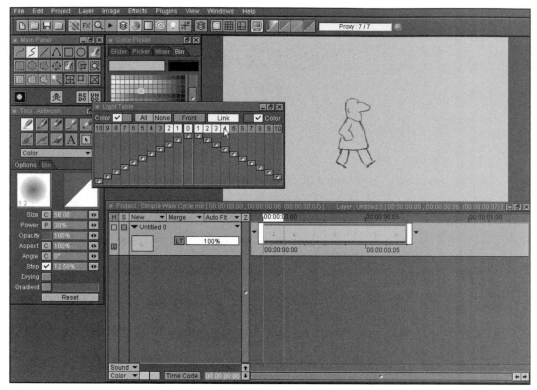

Figure 8.7
The Mirage Studio interface.

3D worlds for your 2D animated characters to run around in, and then add camera-style effects for awesome cinematic-quality cartoons. Toon Boom Studio has publishing options not available in other applications, too, including support for video output to iPods, PDAs, mobiles, HDTV, TV, and the World Wide Web. To see more of the features of Toon Boom Studio and an interactive showcase of work made with it, visit http://www.toonboom.com.

Anime Studio

Anime Studio, formally called Moho, is the application Matt Stone and Trey Parker switched to using to create their Emmy award–winning cartoon series *South Park*. It offers bone-rigging capabilities for 2D characters, helping to speed production time and reduce labor and frustration; you simply point and click to attach bones to your characters for easy manipulation of them in frame-by-frame animation (see Figure 8.9). In addition, Anime Studio has pen-tablet support and a lip-sync system built in. Anime Studio comes with some stock characters

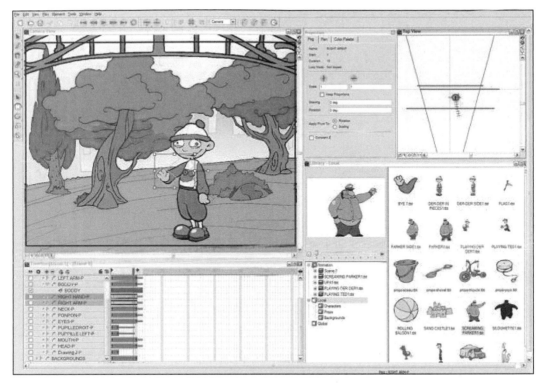

Figure 8.8
The Toon Boom Studio interface.

you can use right away, or through which you can learn the setup and animation structure. One of the most innovative elements of Anime Studio is that you can easily import OBJ files—3D model files made in programs like Poser or Shade—and animate them in Anime Studio. Plus, the tutorials and online community are a boon to users of Anime Studio. To see more of the features of Anime Studio and a gallery of animations made with it, visit http://www.e-frontier.com and click the Anime Studio link.

DigiCel Flipbook

Flipbook (see Figure 8.10) is one of the most trusted pipeline products used by professionals in the animation industry. Flipbook has been used to create such movies as *The Wild Thornberrys Movie, Teacher's Pet, Curious George,* and *The Simpsons Movie.* I first heard of Flipbook because my role model as an artist, Don Bluth, the creator of such films as *The Secret of NIMH, Anastasia,* and *An American Tail,* had switched from working entirely on paper after a long and studied career as an animator to using Flipbook. Flipbook offers several of the

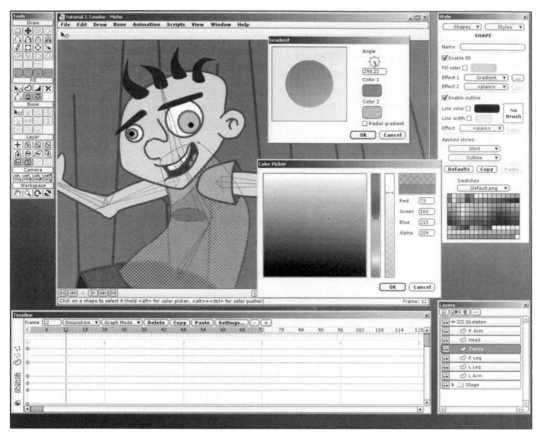

Figure 8.9
Anime Studio is fast for character rigging and manipulation.

features of the aforementioned software packages, including 2D animation, paint, and editing; 3D incorporation and animation; lip-syncing; video integration; and stop-motion animation. You can do rough animation and paperless paper tests before cleaning up and doing your final compositions, all in a very fluid work environment. To see more of Flipbook's features and some demo reels made with it, visit http://www.digicelinc.com.

The Disney Principles

Life is never easy, so why should simulating it in 2D be? Animation is all about bringing characters to life in a vivid imaginary world. Some people have two misconceptions: one, that drawing and animating are easier on computers; and two, that moving stuff around counts as animation. Neither could be further from the truth!

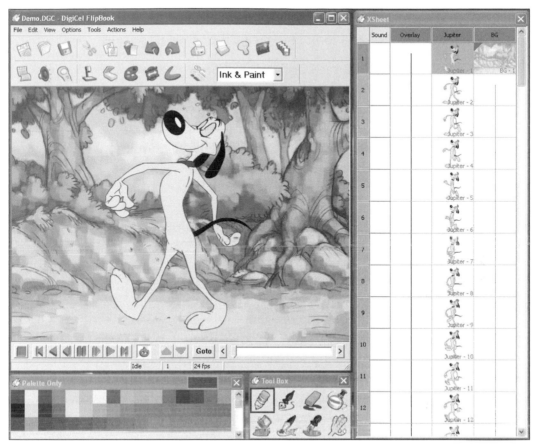

Figure 8.10
The Flipbook interface.

First of all, computers don't do the dirty work for you. Computers may make some tasks easier, but they make others harder. Creating digital art and animations is deliberately slow and tedious whether you choose to do it by hand or with a software application. You have to own a lot of patience to work in animation.

Secondly, making an animated character look good is never quick or easy. Simply moving objects around on your screen does not make animation. Animation is about simulating real actions in an artificial environment, and doing so in a way that is stylish and cool enough to keep the viewer's attention glued.

Therefore, you need some fundamental understanding of animation before you can start. Frank Thomas and Ollie Johnston wrote a book called *The Illusion of Life: Disney Animation,* ratified in the 1930s by Disney Studios; in it, they classified 12 essential principles of animation, which are still used today by professional animators. Let's look at some of the more important ones:

- **Timing.** As mentioned, cartoonists of old drew extremes and then put a number beside them to show how many in-betweens there needed to be between them; all this came from *exposure sheets,* which broke down the animation to the exact screen time each frame would be shown. The number of frames for each pose affects the overall feel of the animation, meaning you must strike the right balance between allowing the action to register with the viewer and creeping along so slowly that you bore your audience. Generally speaking, faster is better, but because computers can make images go by more quickly than the human eye can track them, you run the risk of making your characters blur past too fast.

- **Emphasis.** Emphasis is the process of slowing down and exaggerating the action you want to show in order for audiences to keep up with and understand exactly what is going on. Emphasis also makes for more exciting animation. Indeed, it is arguably the core of truly great cartoons. For example, when a wood chopper chops wood in real life, he moves quickly and decisively, and sometimes his axe can appear to blur by. In a cartoon, however, you don't want that, so you exaggerate the motion. For example, notice in Figure 8.11 how the wood chopper's arms come back, his chest heave out, and his legs strain; then, in the forward swing, the axe whirs by, leaving whiz lines, and goes right through the wood being chopped, and the wood chopper's feet actually leave the ground. This is emphasis.

Figure 8.11
A wood chopper shows several of the Disney principles.

- **Anticipation.** Anticipation is declaring to the viewer what is about to happen before it happens. It sets up the probable action and lets the viewer's eyes drink what comes next. In the wood-chopper example, his exaggerated swing does not start when the axe falls; the action begins with the anticipation, as he brings the axe back over his head and builds the momentum that will result in the downward swing. We time it just right, and the viewer will have no problem imagining what is about to happen. This also adds drama.

- **Follow-through.** Just as a baseball batter does not quit swinging his bat as soon as it hits the baseball and knocks the hide-covered sphere into orbit, the wood chopper doesn't stop his forward movement after his axe taps the wood. Instead, he goes right *through* the wood, and his axe embeds itself in the stump on which he's chopping. Depending on the severity of the blow, it might stop so suddenly that it sends reverberations up his arms and causes his shoulders to shake! Follow-through is about avoiding stopping everything all at once. Related to Newton's law of physics, all things have mass and all objects with mass have momentum. If energy is applied in any given direction, the object will continue in motion until another object repels it or the object exhausts its energy. There should always be some obvious continuation of motion, like cause and effect; otherwise, your animation will look wooden or robotic.

- **Secondary motion.** Secondary motions are smaller, more detailed actions that take place during the main action to support it. They are also called *overlapping actions.* Secondary motions should not override or appear more important than the main action, or else they confuse the viewer. Think of the wood chopper—his hair, clothes, and body parts react to his swing. When he comes for the down-swing, his feet actually leave the ground to show how much force he's putting into his motion. These are all secondary motions, because they are subtle and support the primary motion. Great character animation should clearly communicate to your audience what is going on.

- **Squash and stretch.** Twinkle animation studio co-founder Gary Leib says, "This isn't rocket science, folks. It's more like rubber ball science." And he's right. When something like a rubber ball hits the ground, it squashes flat. When it bounces back up again, it stretches out. It turns spherical just before it starts back toward the ground, in which case it elongates for a second time. Then it will hit the ground and go flat once more. It repeats this cycle until the rubber ball loses forward inertia or it hits another object, like a wall. The repeated process of squash and stretch results in the flexible, fluid, and bouncy objects and characters that you see in cartoons. Practice the bouncing ball exercise in Chapter 2, "Basic Drawing Techniques," to get this principle down pat.

▪ **Weight distribution.** Every existing object shares space, volume, and mass. Keep this in mind, even when drawing and animating comical characters like Wile E. Coyote. Notice that when he is riding an Acme brand rocket and runs into a boulder, his body doesn't scrunch up as skinny as he looks; instead, it flattens out like a pancake or folds up like an accordion. When the rubber ball bounces, in the principle of squash and stretch, it flattens out when it hits the ground and stretches when it leaps through the air. This is because of weight distribution through the object due to vertical mass. You want to make your 2D images carry definite weight because they'll appear more real to your viewer, and the world in which they reside, while never realistic, will appear more convincing as a place.

▪ **Appeal.** Frank Thomas and Ollie Johnston said in their book, "While a live actor has charisma, the animated character has appeal." What they were talking about was that onscreen actors are living beings that come across mostly through their raw magnetism, but you can't emulate this raw magnetism in doodles. Instead, you have to count on your animated characters oozing appeal. Your audience must not mind looking at your drawings and must have a definite psychological connection to them as the action progresses. Use your best judgment when drawing to give your characters adequate appeal.

Spotlight on Jason ''Hot Lips'' Yungbluth

In the words of Jason Yungbluth, "*Deep Fried* is a comic book (at turns, a comic strip) specializing in untouchable comedy subjects. It is written and drawn by me, Jason Yungbluth. *Deep Fried* is a humor anthology featuring recurring characters and assorted one-offs. Frequently returning players include Beepo and Roadkill, Clarissa and Weapon Brown." *Deep Fried* (see Figure 8.12) started in 2000 and has been distributed by Diamond Comics Distributors, Cold Cut, and FM International.

Q. At what age did you get started drawing?

A. Bin drawrin' my whole life.

Q. What inspires you?

Figure 8.12
August 14th, 2006 comic episode of *Deep Fried Weekly*. (Image courtesy Jason Yungbluth, 2006.)

A. Various factors. In political matters, rage does, both at the world and at my own lethargy. In writing, a clever witticism or turn of phrase that I simply must communicate does. Artistically I am always striving to improve my technique or arrive at some new plateau, and I like drawings that put a scar on my readers' eyeballs.

Q. Any beginning-artist tips?

A. Practice makes perfect! Master anatomy.

Q. What's the coolest thing about being a comic artist?

A. Chicks dig artists, and I really love it when I elicit a genuine laugh.

Q. Any other advice for young artists?

A. Work hard and don't give up. Comic art is a competitive field. To last you must love what you do. Draw what gives you joy.

Review

In this chapter, you learned about the history of animation, how cartoons are made, and what software applications are used today. You also looked at the Disney principles guiding animation. Next I'll show you how to animate simple cartoons using Adobe Flash 8.

CHAPTER 9

ANIMATION BASICS IN FLASH 8

Adobe Flash, or simply Flash, refers to both the Adobe Flash Player and the multimedia authoring program used to create content such as web applications, games, and movies. Flash Player is a client application available in most web browsers, and Flash features support for vector and raster graphics, a scripting language called ActionScript, and bidirectional streaming of audio and video. Strictly speaking, Flash is an integrated development environment (IDE), while Flash Player is a virtual machine used to run the Flash files. In contemporary terms, however, "Flash" can refer to the authoring environment, the player, or the application files.

Since its introduction in 1996, Flash technology has become a popular method for adding animation and interactivity to web pages. Several software products, systems, and devices can display Flash files. Flash is the number-one tool used by artists for making animated shorts, webtoons, moving graphics, commercials, full-length films, and online games (see Figure 9.1). Most web sites today have some Flash on them; Flash makes the World Wide Web more interactive and attractive.

Animating in Flash

Flash has strengths and weaknesses, making it better for some things than it is for others. As with most software applications, if you can't get what you want done with one tool, look for another. Toon Boom Studio and some of the other 2D

Figure 9.1
Updated daily, http://www.newgrounds.com is a hosting site for loads of Flash content.

applications are better at pen-tablet drawing and cel painting, for instance. For the animation exercises that follow, I'll be using Adobe Flash 8, but most of the principles and steps are general enough to carry over into whatever animation software you choose to use.

There are two standard ways that you can animate in Flash: employing traditional animation techniques and making use of Flash's library of reusable content. When you look at most webtoons, you'll see that the Flash artists often use both approaches.

Using Traditional Animation Techniques in Flash

One way to animate in Flash is to take a traditional approach, employing the same basic techniques as you would if you were making a flipbook or other old-style animation. You create your artwork and characters frame by frame and scan them in using a digital scanner. From there, you vectorize, colorize, and place them into Flash, where you set them up to play frame by frame. This is tedious and painstaking work, but most animators believe that animations created using this approach look better in the long run.

The downside to this style of animation in Flash is that each image you've scanned becomes a symbol in the Flash library. The more images you use over an entire project, the larger the animation file gets, until eventually it consumes megabytes of valuable storage space—meaning you can't hope to put your movie on the World Wide Web, because people with 56 Kbps download speeds will never be able to see it. It is also a laborious way of animating; it takes time, and there are automated processes that can speed matters along.

Employing Flash's Reusable Content

Another way to animate in Flash is to make use of Flash's built-in library system, where you store reusable symbols. You can place symbols on your stage, position individual exposures on keyframes (which are the drawings that form the starting and end point of a smooth transition in an animation), and interpolate the rest. You can also make use of Flash's guided motion, motion, and shape tweens (snappy digital methods for creating in-betweens) for shortcuts. This is great, because it takes less time drawing your characters and scanning them in, and the final file sizes are portable enough to put on the web.

The downside to this method is that moving objects around or blending from one symbol to another is not really animation, and it can look very wooden—especially when a character turns from a front to a profile view or you want to show a 360-degree pan around a subject. It is also entirely too easy, especially for beginning animators, to limit their work, making only one or two symbols that become redundant placeholders over time. Variety is often the key to making proper animations.

Intermingling Methods

The trick, then, is to know when to cheat and use Flash interpolation, and when to draw your scenes and poses by hand the traditional way. This comes from evaluating the pose needed, the composition that you're after, and what key elements could be recycled from one area of your cartoon to another. If you look at the cartoons on TV that use Flash—such as *The Grim Adventures of Billy and Mandy, Foster's Home for Imaginary Friends,* and *Danny Phantom* (among others)—and the webtoons on sites like Newgrounds.com, you will start to see parts that are commonly reused or retooled over and over, and you will also see places where an entire pose had to be drawn from scratch.

Symbols

A *symbol* is any reusable object created or used in Flash. A symbol can be reused throughout your movie or imported and used in other movies that you make. A copy of a symbol used within your movie is called an *instance*. Instances can have their own individual settings, like color, size, function, and alpha transparency. All the symbols that you can use in your movie are stored in a Flash library, which appears as a long list from which you can drag and drop instances onto your work stage. If you decide to edit a symbol, all instances of that symbol within your movie are automatically edited as well.

Using symbols in your Flash movie is absolutely crucial. A movie's file size depends on the size and number of the graphics used within your Flash movie. Reusing symbols rather than drawing new graphics all the time reduces the file size of your Flash movie, better enabling people to download and view it on the web. That's because a symbol's contents are taken into account and drawn only once—even though your Flash movie may contain thousands of instances of it!

Flash has three types of symbols (see Figure 9.2):

- **Graphics.** Graphic symbols are reusable static images that are used mainly for drawing and animation. These symbols can be bitmap/raster images or vector art. They can be large or small, and can be a combination of separate images grouped together for ease of manipulation.

- **Buttons.** Button symbols are used for timeline navigation and interactivity. They respond to mouse clicks, rollovers or rollouts, and key presses. Each button has different graphic states, such as Up, Over, Down, and Hit, for which you can define different looks. Button symbols aren't typically used in web comics, however, so I won't cover them further here.

- **Movie clips.** Movie-clip symbols are reusable Flash movies with their own timelines, and can be made up of multiple images. Placing a movie clip on your stage is like playing a movie within a movie. The great thing about movie clips is that you can use ActionScript to control their settings.

Figure 9.2
Three types of symbols used in Flash are buttons, graphics, and movie clips.

Note

ActionScript enables you to make Flash interactive and gives you the tools to make Flash games and applications. Because we are not creating interactive content here, we won't discuss ActionScript any further; for more information, visit http://www.senocular.com or http://www.flashkit.com.

Tip

Make it a habit to give your symbols clever and identifiable names from the very start, and use folders to group like symbols. It is easy to wind up with dozens or even hundreds of symbols in a Flash project, which makes it next to impossible to find or edit the one you want. I typically put all my movie clips in one set, all my buttons in one set, and all my graphics in one set, and I take the time to name each one so I'll know what the symbol is without having to click it.

Animation Sequences

When working in Flash, you will find it necessary to create shorter animation sequences within the larger whole. Evaluate the sequence you need to animate based on what is being animated, how it should look as it's animating, and what would be the most efficient animation method overall. Flash offers you many sequence options, including the following:

- **Frame-by-frame animation.** Frame-by-frame animation involves placing symbols on the stage and using the timeline to add keyframes of movement.

You can change out the visible symbols on stage for every keyframe or shift the position of symbols on the stage. (Note that this can result in jerky motion if you're not careful.)

- **Motion tweening.** This technique involves placing a symbol somewhere on the stage, creating a keyframe on the timeline there, and then moving along the timeline to a point sometime later and adding another keyframe in which the symbol's position or some other setting has been changed. You then apply a motion tween to the intervening frames, enabling Flash to interpolate the action that occurs between the keyframes for you.

- **Shape tweening.** Shape tweening is similar to motion tweening, except you use separate symbols, usually vector art, in their own keyframes and add a shape tween between them. The shape tween then attempts to gradually shift the look of one symbol into the shape of the other. This can be a fast and ready way to animate a character's mouth as he or she is talking or show the character's squinty eyes blinking.

- **Guided motion tweening.** This technique uses an invisible guideline, or path, to carry the symbol from one keyframe to the next. In the intervening frames, Flash pushes the symbol a little farther along the path until it gets to the end. This is excellent if you want to animate, say, the arc of a baseball soaring through the air or the zigzag of a UFO in flight.

All these animation sequences can be further edited by adding *slow-in* and *slow-out* values. For example, if you want a car to take off really quickly and then gradually disappear over the horizon, you'd add a high slow-out value. Slow-in and slow-out is nothing new to the animation business; it's been around for years as a staple of proper timing in animation. Flash just makes it easier.

Getting Started with Flash

Now that you know some of the basic components of Flash, it's time to learn about the interface and get you started. If you've worked with Flash before and already feel competent in it, you can jump ahead to the "Making a Fluppet" section, where you'll see how a basic digital puppet is created in Flash.

To start, open Flash by selecting it in the Start menu (Windows) or choosing it in the Finder (Mac), or by double-clicking the Flash shortcut icon on your desktop (if applicable). When it finishes initializing, you'll see a blank canvas, called the *stage,* and several different toolsets surrounding it. A *timeline* appears above the stage; the little blank boxes are empty frames.

Look for the Properties tab at the bottom of the screen. You should see the default settings for the stage, or canvas. For now, pay attention to three things:

- **Canvas size.** You can adjust this by entering the desired values. Because you'll usually work with Flash for web production and for designing animated cartoons, it's a good idea to work at a standard size, like 320 × 240 or 800 × 600.

- **Background color.** You can change this by selecting a color in the Color Picker.

- **Frame rate (frames per second).** Although video production typically requires a frame rate of 24 to 30 fps, a frame rate of 12 will provide adequately smooth motion graphics when working with Flash. Opt for this lower value; the higher the number you enter, the more frames get added to your project—and the larger your movie's file size.

Positioned to the left of the stage is the Tools panel, with buttons that provide access to the most-used tools in Flash. Click the icon that looks like a hand; aptly called the Hand tool, you use it to click and drag the stage around to position it where you like it. The Hand tool comes in handy when you're zoomed way in, working on tiny details, and need to move your canvas to the left or right to get at an area you can't see. Now try drawing something. To begin, click the Oval tool button in the Tools panel to select it; it's the button that contains a white circle surrounded by a black outline. With the Oval tool selected, click and drag on the stage to create an oval shape.

Below the buttons in the Tools panel are two Color Picker boxes. The one with the pencil beside it is the Stroke color (that is, the color of the outline of any shape you draw), and the one with the paint bucket beside it is the Fill color (the color inside the shape you draw). Note that these don't *have* to be set to a color; you can click either one to open its Color Picker and choose the box with the red line through it to set the color to None.

Take a moment to doodle a bit on the Flash stage to explore the various tools available to you. When you're finished, erase what you've done by opening the Edit menu and choosing Clear; you're about to create your first digital puppet using Flash.

Making a Fluppet

Joh Kuramoto, Gary Leib, and Daniel Gray wrote a book in 2001 called *The Art of Cartooning with Flash: The Twinkle Guide to Flash Character Animation* (Sybex). In it, they describe what they call "the Twinkle method," which is, more or less, creating a digital Flash puppet and animating it. Flash puppets, or *fluppets* (as Leib calls them), are animated characters constructed from smaller individual parts.

N o t e

Although some software packages offer bones animation, which makes the creation and manipulation of fluppets easier, Adobe Flash 8 does not.

A fluppet typically is made from separate symbols, like two eyes, one mouth, a head, hair, a torso, clothes, two arms, and two legs. These symbols can then be manipulated to create the illusion of movement. For example, imagine a character like a Powerpuff Girl (see Figure 9.3 for an example). You can rotate her legs to make her look like she's kicking or walking down a street, and you can rotate her arms to make her appear to be swinging or punching with them. You can resize her eyes to make them widen in surprise or shrink in suspicion. You can do all of this by positioning her parts and setting up keyframe animation; as an added bonus, using symbols in this way leads to shorter file sizes and faster uploads and downloads.

You can build a standard fluppet yourself. Rather than recreate this punk girl, however, let's make a Humpty Dumpty (as in the nursery rhyme). A round character, Humpty Dumpty is relatively uncomplicated to draw and animate.

Figure 9.3
This punked version of a Powerpuff Girl is composed of very simple shapes that can be easily compiled in Flash.

You'll set up Humpty to walk along a wall, step off of it, and fall to the ground—where Humpty (poor fellow) will crack apart. It will be a short cartoon we'll call *The Short Tragic Fall of Humpty Dumpty*. Sound good? Okay, let's get started!

Creating Symbols

Begin by composing a symbol for Humpty Dumpty's head and body. Since his head and body are one and the same (a giant egg), you don't even need to make them separate symbols. Rather than composing your symbols in Flash, do so by drawing them on paper, inking and polishing them as you go.

Note

> When deciding what needs to be a symbol and what doesn't, you first consider whether the objects are part of the same shape. Then consider whether the objects will ever move independently of each other. If the objects are radically different in shape or if they are animated separately from each other, then you will have to construct them independently.

Draw the Humpty Dumpty head and body as seen in Figure 9.4. You don't have to copy it verbatim; instead, try to come up with your own version of what you think Humpty should look like using Figure 9.4 as your guide. Notice that he does not have eyes or a mouth; I'll get to those in a minute.

Figure 9.4
What Humpty Dumpty's head and body could look like.

If you wanted Humpty to turn from left to right or look up or look down, you'd have to draw separate heads and bodies for Humpty for every frame where the shape would change during the course of his movement. (Remember when you looked at how a face appears different depending on the angle?) You're not concerned with Humpty looking around in this short clip, however. You just want him to walk straight forward. He will, however, crack and fall apart when he hits the ground. For that, you need to make shell fragments.

To make the shell fragments, start with the body shape and separate it along fault or crack lines. When they are put together, they look like Humpty's body; but they can be animated separately so they fall to pieces. If you have Photoshop, you can use the Polygonal lasso tool to select a piece of the main body. First, go Edit > Cut. Then go File > New and choose Clipboard as your preset to make a new file. When the new file is open, go Edit > Paste to paste your shell fragment on the stage; then save the file as an individual GIF or PNG, making sure that you preserve transparency. Of course, you don't have to do this in Photoshop. There may be easier ways to make the shell fragments. This is just the way I did it for this exercise.

Next, create Humpty Dumpty's limbs. The legs will pump along under him as he walks; to show proper distribution of weight, they should bend a little under him when he steps. To depict this, you'll have to use frame-by-frame animation, providing drawings of his legs at different points in his walk cycle. To that end, draw 12 individual symbols that look like the legs in Figure 9.5.

You could do the same with his arms, but you can probably get away with using only two symbols for the walk cycle. You will, however, need additional drawings for the arms for use when the figure falls (see Figure 9.6).

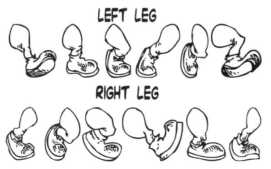

Figure 9.5
Humpty's legs.

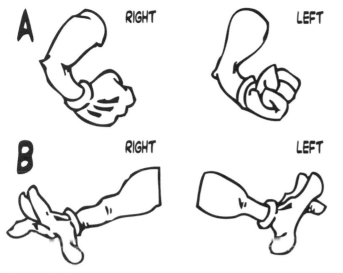

Figure 9.6
Humpty's arms during his walk cycle (A) and when he falls (B).

Figure 9.7
Humpty's expressions can vary widely during the course of the animation.

Last, you need to think about Humpty's expressions, which will be composed of his eyes and mouth. I suggest you work on several hand-drawn versions of Humpty's expressions from scratch and see what you can come up with. You'll need one drawing of him looking normal for when he's just walking along, but you'll also need him looking scared for when he falls off the wall. Then, as a humorous touch, you can make him look sorry for himself after he's been cracked. Take a look at examples in Figure 9.7 and try to guess which expressions are which.

Importing Your Images into Flash

When you are finished drawing all the symbols on paper and you have inked them and polished them as much as you can, you are ready to import them into Flash—almost. First, you need to do the following:

1. Scan the drawings into your computer to convert them into a digital format you can work with.

2. After they have been scanned, import them into a program such as Adobe Photoshop or Illustrator.

3. Optionally, color the images, as discussed in Chapter 5, "Comics Layout and Language." Alternatively, you can opt to stick with black-and-white illustrations, as I've done in this example.

4. Separate each illustration into its own file. For example, rather than having a single file that contains all the drawings of the character's legs, save each leg drawing separately in its own file. To achieve this, use the Crop tool to select a single leg drawing and save it.

Note

When saving your images, provide each one with a meaningful and distinct name. For example, you might use rleg01 as the name for the first drawing of the right leg in the walk cycle. That way, when you need to find or edit that image, you'll be able to locate it easily.

5. To prevent your images from appearing square in Flash—i.e. as a drawing with a square white background—erase the background of each image in Photoshop (or a similar program), making it transparent. Then save each image as a GIF file, preserving the transparency.

6. Next, use Adobe Illustrator CS2's Live Trace feature to convert your images into vector art. This simplifies both the colors and the line drawings themselves, so be prepared for the possibility of some pretty radical differences.

Note

Another approach is to use the Trace Bitmap option when importing the images into Flash to convert them into vector art. A Color Threshold of 25 and a Minimum Area of 1 pixel with a Curve Fit set to Smooth should do the trick. Then delete any background using Flash's Eraser tool or by clicking the background and pressing the Delete key.

Now you're ready to import your images into Adobe Flash for use as symbols. To do so, open the File menu, choose Import, select Import to Library, and select each piece of artwork separately. You should have one egg shape, 12 legs, four arms, five or more eggshell fragments, and as many faces as you deemed appropriate.

Creating Animation Sequences

After you import all the images into Flash, you are ready to turn them into symbols that Flash can use. You'll begin by making a movie-clip symbol of Humpty walking, which you'll add to your scene a bit later.

Tip

Save your Flash file now and often! Make sure that your hard work's been backed up.

Walk Animation

To create the walk animation movie-clip symbol, do the following:

1. Drag an instance of the egg body to the stage.

2. Right-click the egg and select Create Symbol from the menu that appears.

3. Choose Movie Clip as the symbol type, and name the symbol Humpty Walk. Then click OK.

4. Double-click this new movie clip symbol. Notice that you're no longer in Scene 1, but that you've entered Humpty Walk.

5. Double-click the Layer 1 name and rename it Body.

6. Right-click an empty space on the animation and select Insert Layer from the menu that appears.

7. Name the new layer Right Leg.

8. With the Right Leg layer selected, drag an instance of the first frame of animation of the right leg, which you might've named rleg01, to the stage.

9. Repeat steps 6–8 to add the following layers to our Humpty Walk timeline, naming each layer appropriately:

   - The left leg (first frame of animation). Name this layer Left Leg.

   - The right arm (use the bent-elbow one, for walking). Name this layer Right Arm.

- The left arm (use the bent-elbow one, for walking). Name this layer Left Arm.

- A facial expression. Name this layer Face.

10. Click the Left Leg layer and drag it below the Body layer in the timeline hierarchy. This places Humpty's left leg behind his body, but makes it still visible around his round shape.

Note

The layers on the timeline not only separate individual and opposite animations, they also perform the same role as the layers within Photoshop.

11. Repeat step 10 with the Left Arm layer.

12. If necessary, drag the Right Arm and Right Leg layers above the Body layer, and place the Face layer at the very top (see Figure 9.8).

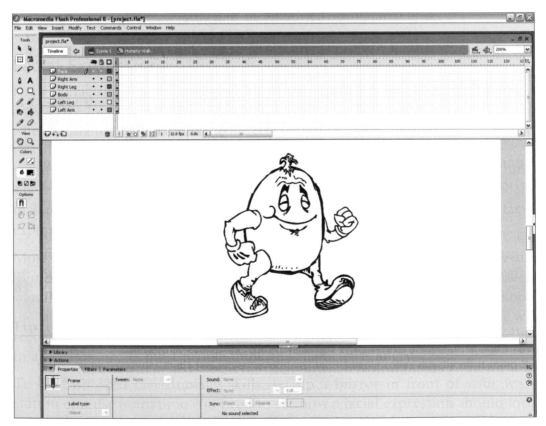

Figure 9.8
Humpty Walk's setup.

13. Right-click the first frame of the Right Leg layer's timeline and select Create Motion Tween.

14. Move over two frames, to frame 3, on that layer's timeline, right-click, and select Insert Keyframe. The timeline turns purple and an arrow appears between the two black dots; the black dots signify keyframes that have items on them.

15. Move over one frame, to frame 4, on that layer's timeline, right-click, and select Insert Blank Keyframe. Instead of a black dot, you should see an empty dot.

16. With frame 4's blank keyframe selected, and making sure you're still on the Right Leg layer, drag an instance of your second frame of the right leg animation, which you might've named rleg02, from your Library onto the stage. Be sure to place it in roughly the same spot as the right leg image you had before it.

Tip

Click the Onion Skin button below the timeline to see several frames of animation at once. This overlay effect will assist you in proper placement of symbol instances. You will likely have to turn Onion Skin on and off occasionally as you work.

17. Go back to frame 3 and select the leg instance.

18. Using the Free Transform tool (hotkey Q), move and rotate the leg in frame 3 to an in-between position, between the first keyframe and the instance of the second leg symbol.

19. Repeat steps 15–18, adding subsequent right leg symbols every third keyframe, until all six right-leg symbols have been added. You should fill a total of 18 frames, which will take a little over a second to play.

20. Repeat steps 13–19 with the left leg, using all six leg symbols and up to 18 frames with a new leg symbol placed on the stage every third frame (see Figure 9.9).

Tip

You can click and drag along the top of the timeline, where the numbers are, to *scrub* through the animation and preview your work. Scrubbing means that you can preview the frames in quick succession, similar to how it will look when you view the animation later. Fine-tune both your left and right legs so that the animation is as close to flawless as you can get.

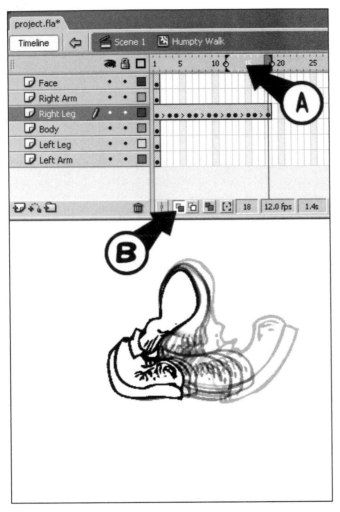

Figure 9.9
Setting up keyframes for a motion tween. A: The frame numbers on the timeline; B: The Onion Skin button.

21. To animate the swing of the arms, begin by selecting the Right Arm layer.

22. Right-click frame 1 and select Create Motion Tween.

23. Right-click frame 9 and choose Insert Keyframe.

24. Right-click frame 18 and choose Insert Keyframe.

25. Using the Free Transform tool (hotkey Q), move and rotate the arm in frame 9 so that it appears to have swung backward.

26. Repeat steps 21–25 on the Left Arm layer, but this time use the Free Transform tool to move and rotate the arm in frame 9 so that it appears to have swung forward and up.

27. Click the Face layer. You might notice that you have 18 frames of animation in our other layers, but the Face layer only has one; as such, the face image would disappear in the blink of an eye.

28. Right-click frame 18 and select Insert Frame (there's no need for a keyframe right now). This allows the face to remain visible for the duration of the animation.

29. If your face overlaps your right arm when the arm's swinging, drag the Right Arm layer above the Face layer in the layer hierarchy so that the face remains behind the arm. Layer order is just as important as it is in 2D art programs like Photoshop for handling the visibility and appearance of each layer.

30. To bring your egg body back, because it won't be visible past frame 1, right-click frame 18 on the Body layer and select Insert Frame. This extends its visible time.

Tip

When you're more experienced with Flash, you might add a wobble to the body so that it doesn't appear to glide. For now, though, you shouldn't worry about it.

31. With all the layers visible up to frame 18, scrub through the animation to preview it. Compare your work with Figure 9.10. If you see anything that seems a little off, now is the time to fix it.

32. Last but not least, consider adding a shadow beneath the egg. To begin, create another layer and name it Shadow.

33. In the Oval layer, use the Oval tool to create an ellipse on the ground under Humpty's feet. The shape should not have any stroke color, but its fill color should be black.

34. Right-click the oval and convert it into a graphic symbol, naming it shadow_gr.

35. Move the Shadow layer to the very bottom of the timeline hierarchy so that it physically lies beneath Humpty.

36. With shadow_gr selected, go to the Properties panel and set its color to Alpha 20%. This will reduce the opaqueness of the shadow.

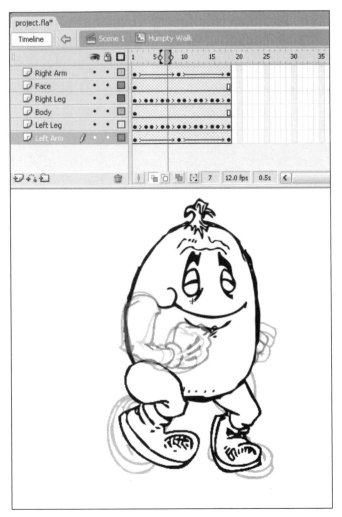

Figure 9.10
Humpty Walk (with Onion Skin turned on).

Humpty may appear to walk in place, but that's all you need for now! In the next chapter, I'll show you how to take this movie clip and put it in a scene.

Humpty Fall

To exit the Humpty Walk movie clip symbol and return to Scene 1, either click the next region up in your Flash file above the timeline or double-click somewhere off to the side of your stage, wherever your symbol isn't. After you exit the Humpty Walk movie clip, delete the instance you see of it on the stage. This won't delete all your hard work, because the movie clip is now stored in your Library; it just clears your workspace so that you can continue working.

You're going to create a new movie clip to illustrate Humpty falling. Here's how:

1. Drag an instance of the body symbol to the stage.

2. Right-click the body symbol and select Create Symbol from the menu that appears.

3. Choose Movie Clip as the symbol type, and name the symbol Humpty Fall. Click OK.

4. Double-click this new movie-clip symbol. Notice that you're no longer in Scene 1, but that you've entered Humpty Fall.

5. Double-click the Layer 1 name and rename it Body.

6. On the Body layer, drag one instance each of the right and left legs to the stage and arrange them around the body so they look like they're raised a little in the air. In order to do this, you will have to use the Free Transform tool (hotkey Q) to rotate them.

7. Rather than moving the left leg to a separate layer to move it so that it sits behind the egg body, right-click the left leg, choose Arrange, and select Send to Back. The left leg should hide neatly behind the egg body.

Note

You only use layers for elements you want to animate separately. Because we're not animating the legs separate from the body, there's no real need to put them in separate layers.

8. Now you need to create a new layer for the left arm. Right-click the Body layer on the timeline and select Insert Layer from the menu that appears.

9. Name the new layer Left Arm.

10. With the Left Arm layer selected, drag an instance of the left arm (falling) to the stage.

11. Repeat steps 8–10 to add the following instances to the stage, naming each layer appropriately:

    ■ The right arm (falling). Name this layer Right Arm.

    ■ A facial expression of surprise. Name this layer Face.

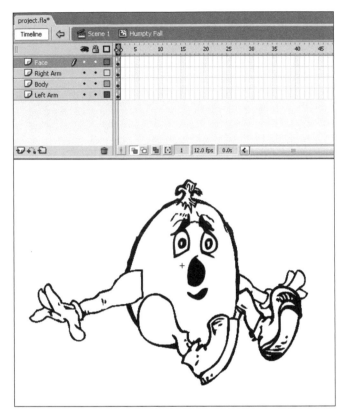

Figure 9.11
A screenshot of Humpty Fall's setup.

12. You will want to do the same thing with the left arm that you did before—that is, move the Left Arm layer beneath the Body layer so that it is half-hidden by the body. Likewise, move the Face layer to the top of the layer stack (see Figure 9.11).

13. Use what you learned in the previous section to animate the fall. Experiment! Now that you know how motion tweening works, move the arms up and down so that it looks like Humpty is waving them or trying to fly. Your animation doesn't have to be 18 frames long; in fact, given the height of the wall, your fall animation should be less than a second. As you can see in Figure 9.12, I created a 12-frame-long animation. If the fall lasts longer than that, the movie clip will loop.

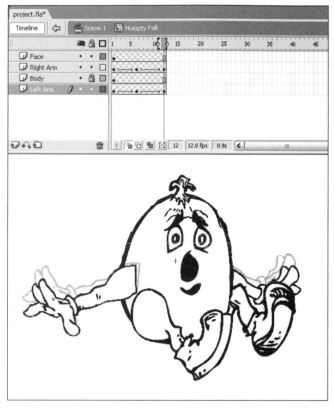

Figure 9.12
Humpty Fall (with Onion Skin turned on).

Note

You can lock certain layers so that you don't mess them up or so that you can access hard-to-get elements on layers behind or beneath them. To do so, find the lock icon on the timeline and layers hierarchy and click the box beneath it on the layer that you want locked. A lock graphic will then appear on the layer that's locked. To unlock the layer, click the box beneath the lock icon again. Likewise, you can hide/unhide layers by clicking the box under the layer's eyeball icon.

Humpty Crack

You're ready to create the animation of Humpty cracking. As before, exit the movie clip you just created and return to Scene 1. Then do the following (Figure 9.13 shows the finished setup):

1. Drag an instance of the body symbol to the stage.

2. Right-click the body symbol and select Create Symbol from the menu that appears.

Figure 9.13
Humpty Crack's setup.

3. Choose Movie Clip as the symbol type, and name the symbol Humpty Crack. Click OK.

4. Double-click this new movie-clip symbol. Notice that you're no longer in Scene 1, but that you've entered Humpty Crack.

5. Double-click the Layer 1 name and rename it Body.

6. Right-click the Body layer in the timeline and select Insert Layer from the menu that appears.

7. Name the new layer Shell1.

8. With the Shell1 layer selected, drag an instance of a shell fragment to the stage and arrange it over the top of the body so that it looks like it fits in place where it would go if it were part of his eggshell.

9. Repeat steps 6–8 to add several new layers to your timeline using the remaining shell fragments, naming them Shell2, Shell3, etc.

10. Next, add the following layers and their symbol instances to your timeline.:

   ■ Using the Paintbrush tool, draw hashes (like this: > <) for his eyes. Name this layer Face.

   ■ The right arm (use the bent-elbow one, for walking). Name this layer Right Arm.

   ■ The right leg (use the same right-leg symbol as the one used in Humpty Fall). Name this layer Right Leg.

Note

By the way, the reason you are creating separate layers for the legs this time is because you want the shell fragments, which will be animated, to be between the right and left leg where the body was before. In order to do this, you must arrange them on separate layers and be very careful about layer order.

   ■ The left arm (use the bent-elbow one, for walking). Name this new layer Left Arm.

   ■ The left leg (use the same left-leg symbol as the one used in Humpty Fall). Name this new layer Left Leg.

11. If you haven't already, arrange the shell layers on the stage so the shell fragments appear in the original egg shape.

Tip

If you have a hard time seeing where the eggshells should go because of the white on white, consider changing the background color to a deeper color. You can always change it back later.

12. Drag the Left Leg layer behind the Body and Shell layers in the timeline.

13. Repeat step 12 with the Left Arm layer.

14. If necessary, drag the Right Arm and Right Leg layers above the Body layer in the timeline, and place the Face layer at the very top.

Note

As you've probably noticed, this is very close to the other animation states you've already done. If you're comfortable with Flash, you could duplicate one of those earlier movie clips and rearrange elements to suit this one.

15. Position Humpty so he's sitting like he's just landed on the ground.

16. Right-click frame 6 of the Body layer and choose Insert Frame from the menu that appears. After this frame, his body will no longer appear.

17. Starting at frame 8 on each shell fragment layer, create a short (maybe 12-frames-long) motion tween in which the fragments fall away from the body, half-rolling to the ground around Humpty. Given that the shell fragments are on separate layers and are in different spots in the layer order, some of them can cover others. Make it look like a tangled mess.

18. Add a motion tween to the arms such that they fall to his side horizontally to the ground. (The legs should remain where they were.)

19. Right-click frame 8 of the Face layer and choose Insert Blank Keyframe.

20. Using the Paintbrush tool, draw a pair of unhappy-looking eyes, based on your original paper drawing, for Humpty's face. The reason you don't want to use a symbol here is because you are going to add a shape tween, and shape tweens only work between a set of vector shapes. Your hash marks you drew earlier are a vector shape, and these eyes will be a vector shape as well.

21. Click frame 6 of the Face layer. Then, in the Properties panel, change the Tween setting to Shape. This adds a shape tween from the hash marks to the unhappy eyes.

Note

The timeline's background turns green when you apply a shape tween. When motion tweens are applied, it turns purple.

22. Wait 12 or so frames, and then repeat steps 19–21 to add a blink or to change to different eyes, like pitiful or sad ones.

Note

As you can see, shape tweens are very useful for making eyes blink. They are also handy for making small mouths talk. With experience, you can actually construct a lip-sync to playable sound effects, using the shape tweens to move from one lip formation to another as a character talks. Note that shape tweens demand that any symbols used be vector art.

23. Add a final layer, called Action.

24. Open the Actions panel. By default, this panel is hidden above the Properties panel, at the bottom of the Flash interface. If you don't see it, call it by opening the Window menu and choosing Actions.

25. Create a keyframe at the very end of your animation. For me, this was frame 46.

26. With this new keyframe selected, type the following in the Actions panel to freeze the animation, preventing it from looping (see Figure 9.14):

```
stop();
```

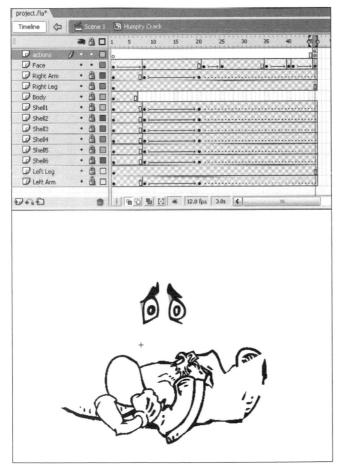

Figure 9.14
The last of poor Humpty Dumpty.

Review

In this chapter, you opened Adobe Flash, learned about its basic interface and components, and created a digital puppet that you can animate. Using the knowledge you gained in Chapter 8, "Principles of Animation," you could make Humpty Dumpty's animation more detailed, adding subtle nuances and your own signature style. Much of perfection is the result of experience, so the more animations you make in Flash, the better you will get at it—and the better your results. You'll look at finishing your animated short film *The Short Tragic Fall of Humpty Dumpty* in the next chapter.

CHAPTER 10

BUILDING SCENES

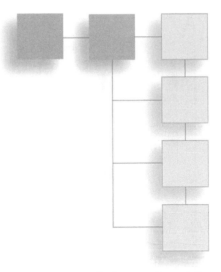

You've gotten your feet wet animating now. You have started the project *The Short and Tragic Fall of Humpty Dumpty* by making several movie clips, or *interior animations,* of the ever-popular nursery rhyme egg-man Humpty walking, falling, and cracking apart. Now I'll show you how to put the scene together.

Creating Backgrounds

Setting is just as important in a good story as character. Really, setting can be another type of character—albeit limited in the form of interactions it can provide the viewer. Some people like stories that are set in far-off lands and places they'd like to visit on their vacations. Other people like stories set some place welcoming and familiar, like their own backyard.

Designing a Background

When you design a background for your comics or your toons, you need to keep it clear in your mind that the action doesn't take place in a vacuum. There has to be some indication of *setting*—that is, where the action is taking place—so that the viewer can immerse himself or herself in it.

Charles Schulz, the creator *Peanuts,* one of the longest-running strips of its time, often didn't draw in backgrounds to his comic strips. Instead, he added a line or a

Figure 10.1
The clear style of one comic image (A) and the heavier, more detailed style of another (B).

few small details that would cement the setting conceptually and let the rest fade to white or some off-white color. He did this intentionally; indeed, he made his characters just as simple as his backgrounds, with very few illuminating details about what they looked like. On the other end of the spectrum you see artists like the ones who do the *Batman* comic books. These artists create endless amounts of detail and sweeping vistas of Gotham, and blend it all with dark impenetrable shadows. This visual choice is really an artist's decision. What do you want to convey, and how do you want to convey it? Consider this carefully before you draw backgrounds for your comic panels or empty animation stages. Figure 10.1 shows both an example of a minimalized comic image and a more complex image.

For this project, let's make an outdoor scene. There should be a wall, a sky, and some ground. How it looks is up to you. You could add a sun or clouds to your sky, draw some trees and bushes, add some mountains to the background, and even create some rocks in the foreground. You could add a barn or other building to the background, and your wall could be made of stone, brick, or some combination of the two. However you draw it, your background should be made to the same scale that you designed your character. Even though you can scale objects in Flash to make them look bigger, you will still not be able to change the line width of your line drawings. So when you're drawing everything on paper, prior to digital scanning, try to draw at the scale you'd imagine the background to be in relation to the characters. You can see my example in Figure 10.2.

Figure 10.2
One example of a background you could draw for your project.

When you get really good at animating images and working with nested movie clips, you can add animated details to your backgrounds. For instance, a squirrel could sit, gnawing a nut, on the limb of a tree, while the tree's branches sway in the wind. Clouds could scuttle across the sky. The sun could have a large happy face that changes to an unhappy face when Humpty falls. The possibilities, once you start thinking like an animator, are virtually endless.

Note

Many backgrounds will require characters to walk behind or over objects that exist as part of the background. Characters may have to walk through doorways, stoop behind boulders, or cross in front of a chair in a living room. When this happens, you can either make the objects separate to start with or trace a copy of the objects. Either way, you'll have to place them on a layer higher than the rest in the timeline hierarchy. A more advanced Flash user could also use layer masks, but we won't go into that in this book, as it is a slightly more complicated (though equally effective) technique.

Putting Your Background on the Stage

Scan in your background artwork. If you wish, you can use a paint-editing program to color it or clean it up. You may also want to vectorize your raster image for a smoother appearance using either Adobe Illustrator's Live Trace function or Adobe Flash's Trace Bitmap function. It's up to you. When you get through with your background, import it to your Flash project's library. Be sure to give it a distinct name like background or BG. Then do the following:

1. Create a new layer in Scene 1 and call it BG.

2. Move the BG layer to the very bottom of your layer hierarchy, under Layer 1.

3. Make sure the BG layer is selected, then drag an instance of your background graphic to the stage.

4. Use the Align options now to align the background correctly on the stage. Specifically, be sure the Align/Distribute to Stage button (A in Figure 10.3) is highlighted and active and click the Align to Horizontal Center button (B in Figure 10.3) and the Align to Vertical Center button (C in Figure 10.3) to center the background image to the stage. If it looks right, you might click the Match Screen Height/Width button (D in Figure 10.3) to make sure your background graphic fills up the stage; if it looks wrong, or the line widths exceed acceptable parameters, go Edit > Undo.

ALIGN PANEL

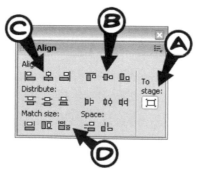

Figure 10.3
The Align panel. A: Align/Distribute to Stage button; B: Align to Horizontal Center button; C: Align to Vertical Center button; D: Match Screen Height/Width button.

Note

If you do not see your Align options on the screen (by default, they appear on the right side of the interface), open the Window menu and select Align.

Your camera, which is your current field of view (FOV), won't change during this short animated movie, so you don't have much to worry about there. You could have made the wall seem taller and had the background run off the stage; then, during Humpty's fall, you'd animate the background to raise it up the stage until you could see the ground. Better yet, you could add a motion blur to the wall in between. But we'll stick to something simple right now. You can add to your movie as your experience with the software grows. Humpty won't have to walk in front of or move behind any of the objects in this background, either. Otherwise, you'd have to set up those objects on separate layers and move them above Layer 1 and sort them by depth.

Animating the Scene

To animate the scene, do the following:

1. Rename Layer 1 to Animations.

2. Place an instance of the Humpty Walk movie clip on the Animations layer at the top of the wall on the left side of the stage.

3. Delete any other symbol instances remaining on this layer.

Note

Your movie clip won't show up as animated. Instead, it shows the first frame of an animation. You won't see the actual animation until you test the movie as a whole.

4. Right-click the first frame of the Animations layer and choose Create Motion Tween. (Motion tweens allow you to interpolate action from one keyframe to another seamlessly, so you don't have to draw every in-between frame by hand.)

5. Insert a keyframe on frame 15 and a blank keyframe on frame 16.

6. On frame 15, nudge the Humpty Walk movie clip to the very edge of the wall. *Nudging* means to use only the arrow keys (or the Shift and arrow keys) to move objects either straight horizontally or vertically.

7. On frame 16, where you placed the blank keyframe, drag an instance of the Humpty Fall movie clip. Make sure that it's approximately the same size and location of the last frame of Humpty Walk.

8. The motion tween you set earlier should persist, meaning the timeline on that layer will be highlighted and filled with arrows or dashed lines, so click frame 25 and insert a keyframe. Then insert a blank keyframe on frame 26.

9. You guessed it: On frame 25, nudge the Humpty Fall instance straight down to the ground, and add the final animation, Humpty Crack, on frame 26.

10. Insert a frame on frame 65 for both the BG and Animations layers.

11. Insert a new layer and call it Action.

12. Insert a keyframe on frame 65 of the Action layer and, just as you did with the last frame of the Humpty Crack movie clip, type stop(); in the Actions panel to force the animation to stop.

13. Test your movie by opening the Control menu and choosing Test Movie. A Flash Player will open your movie, showing how it will look when it is published and enabling you to preview it. If the animation seems glitchy or the speed of one of the nested movie clips doesn't compare with the speed of the overall project, then this is when you're going to notice it and make the appropriate changes.

That's it! Pat yourself on the back. You've successfully completed an entire animation process from start to finish. This was just an experiment to help you learn the interface and the process by which webtoons are created. Now that you have built one webtoon, you have the wherewithal to build many more. But before you do, I want to discuss two important issues with webtoons: adding sound effects and titles.

Adding Sound Effects

According to Peter Sylwester, writer for Songline Productions, "Toss a rock into the river. The splash consists of two things—the impact we see and the impact we hear. The impact we see sends ripples across the water; the impact we hear is from ripples in the air. A little rock produces little ripples and a little sound. A big rock produces big ripples and a big sound. The sound validates the impact . . . Sound describes what we see. Stop and listen; sound also describes what we don't see. Sound accompanies us and can tell us where we are and who we're with."

Sound forms a full fifth of the way we perceive our environment, and we innately use sound as a means of survival. Being capable of telling when a noisy ambush predator like a cougar snuck up behind our ancestors helped them stay alive—and today we use sound to listen to the latest pop hits on our iPods. Watch a YouTube video without headphones or a speaker and realize just how disappointing the experience quickly becomes.

Sound comes in the shape of vibration waves. Some sound waves can actually travel at frequencies so high or low that humans cannot hear them, but some animals can (such as the dog hearing a dog whistle).

Here are some of the most basic laws of sound:

- A sound wave moves pretty much in a straightforward fashion.

- *Pitch* refers to how quickly the sound wave vibrates, also known as *frequency*. Humans can discern sound frequencies by a 2:1 difference, so many of our music notes are on a scale of 2.

- The term hertz (Hz) comes from a unit of frequency equaling one vibration per second.

- Humans can hear between 20 hertz (Hz) and approximately 20,000 Hz (or 20 kHz).

- *Intensity* is how loud the sound comes across, also called *amplitude* or *volume*. Intensity is measured in decibels (dB). The increasing intensity of a sound wave is known as *gain*.

- *Timbre* is the waveform or accuracy of the sound frequency. Timbre is different for every instrument and every voice, and reflects a change in quality that is not dependent on intensity or frequency.

Flash sound involves one of three digital audio file formats: WAV, MP3, and OGG. MP3 and OGG files are compressed audio files, while WAV files are uncompressed, meaning they can be quite large—and, as a result, because they contain more sound information, typically sound pretty good. The quality of a WAV file is determined by how well it was originally recorded. Generally, you'll work with WAV files for sound, but do be aware that they can take up quite a lot of room in memory.

Compression restricts the range of sound by attenuating signals exceeding a threshold. By attenuating louder signals, you limit the dynamic range of sound to existing signals. Imagine that the digital audio file is a piece of paper with sheet notes on it. Compressing it is literally wadding up the piece of paper into a tiny ball. To listen to the music in its compressed state, you have to use a device like an MP3 player to un-wad and smooth out the piece of paper. The most popular compressed audio file on the market right now (made popular by iPods and other MP3 players) is the MP3. Ogg Vorbis is the format of choice on Linux and AIFF for Macintosh. OGG files use a different (and some say better) encoding process to compress the audio. If you've never heard of OGG files before, check out www.vorbis.com for more information.

You could record and play a sound effect of the eggshell cracking or of Humpty saying "Oops!" when he falls. Audacity is a free, open-source software application you can use to record and edit sounds. It is available online for Mac OSX, Windows, and Linux at http://audacity.sourceforge.net. Audacity handles most audio file types, including the same ones Flash uses; and if you use the Lame Encoder you can use Audacity even to edit MP3s. For the purposes of our project, however, it might be better to find a pre-existing snippet of music and play it in the background. Following are online sources for royalty-free music and sound effects that you can incorporate directly into Flash:

- **Bbm.net (http://www.bbm.net)**

- **DeusX.com (http://www.deusx.com/studio.html)**

- **Flashsound.com (http://www.flashsound.com)**

- **Flashkit.com (http://www.flashkit.com)**

- **Killersound.com (http://www.killersound.com)**

- **Shockwave-Sound.com (http://shockwave-sound.com)**

- **Soundrangers.com (http://www.soundrangers.com)**

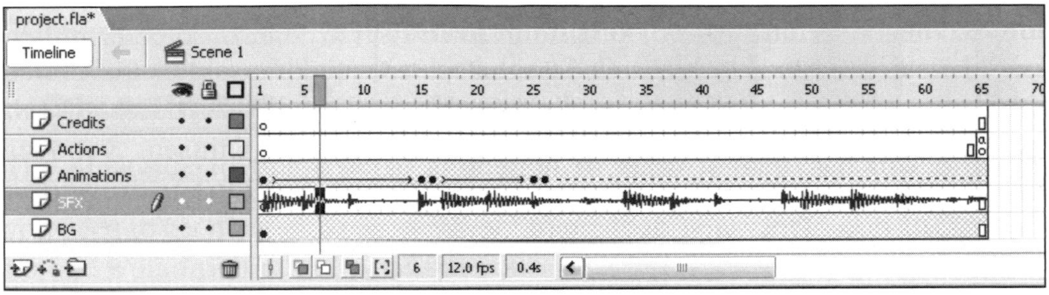

Figure 10.4
A waveform shows up in the Flash timeline after sound is added to the stage.

Regardless of whether you choose to record your own sound or to use one of the sounds available online, you must import it into your Flash library. To do so, open the File menu, choose Import, and select Import to Library; then find the digital audio file you wish to import. After it's been imported, it shows up in your library as a separate symbol type; you can actually play it from the library to hear how it will sound.

Then, to set up the sound to play continuously throughout your project, follow these simple steps:

1. Create a new layer and call it SFX.

2. In the first frame of this new layer, in the Properties panel, select Sound and find the sound you've just imported to your Flash Library—or simply drag an instance of the sound to the stage.

3. When the waveform becomes visible in the timeline, as in Figure 10.4, change the Sync setting in the Properties panel from the default, Repeat, to Loop to make sure that the sound never stops.

4. Sound in Flash can play in dual channels, and there are lots of editing options built into Flash to distort sound along these two channels. Scan these in the Effect drop-down list or click the Custom button; experiment with the settings to see what sounds best.

Note

You can play multiple sounds in a single Flash scene. Just place each sound on a separate layer to make editing easier.

Note

The waveform you see onscreen in the Flash timeline is an aid to you when you start syncing character animations to recorded dialog. Study your mouth in the mirror and practice saying the same lines as the recorded dialog, and look for the same pitch changes on the timeline to know where to put those animation frames. Most webtoon viewers are very forgiving when it comes to lip syncing, however, so don't freak out if it's not perfect.

Adding Titles

You will almost certainly want to set up a title screen and an end credits screen for your animation. This is best done with rapid fade-ins and fade-outs, although it can be done in any other fashion you can dream up. You can go online to see some excellent examples of title animations—which are often not recognized for the art form they are—created by other artists at Forget the Film: Watch the Titles (www.submarinechannel.com/titlesequences). Most title animations for movies are made with Flash or After Effects. The best ones have multiple layers and nested animations.

To create your title animation, do the following:

1. Make a start screen. I'm going to use an original illustration with a thick black vignette around it (see Figure 10.5). You can draw your own or make it out of composite elements. It should match the stage height and width and be centered to the stage, and it should be converted to a graphic symbol called titlescreen.

2. Create a new layer and name it Title.

3. Drag an instance of the titlescreen graphic symbol to the Title layer.

4. Right-click the Title layer's timeline and set a motion tween, but don't move the titlescreen symbol. Instead, go to frame 5 and set a keyframe. Then, in the Properties panel, set the Color value to Alpha 0%. This sets up a very basic fade, where the titlescreen image will fade until it's invisible.

5. If you can't see the Scenes panel, call it forth by opening the Window menu and choosing Other Panels (hotkey: Shift+F2). Flash defaults to a single scene, called Scene 1.

6. Double-click Scene 1, which is where you created your content, and call it Content.

Figure 10.5
An example of a title screen for *The Short Tragic Fall of Humpty Dumpty.*

7. Select your titlescreen symbol on the stage, frame 1, and copy it (press Ctrl+C for Win, Cmd+C for Mac).

8. Click the Add Scene button on the Scenes panel and name this new scene Intro.

9. Click and drag to move Intro above the Content scene in the Scenes hierarchy, so that it will come first.

10. Right-click the stage inside Intro and from the pop-up options select Paste in Place.

11. Right-click the frame 35 on the timeline and select Insert Frame. This gives the viewer 35 frames to read the title before it fades away and the animation starts.

Additionally, you could add an credits animation scene at the end of your movie and call it Credits. You'd transition from the Content scene to the Credits scene the same way you faded from the Intro to the Content scene, or you could experiment with different types of transitions.

Note

> One kind of transition you see a lot in Flash is animated wipes. You can create a short movie clip consisting of painted blobs that fill up the space over several frames, with a `stop()`; on the final frame of the animation. You'd place this movie clip on a layer immediately above the layer you want to transition to, right-click the layer you want to transition to, and select Mask. This uses the movie clip as a layer mask; anywhere there's paint, you should see the layer beneath show up.

Publishing

Test your movie again to make sure everything looks great. Compare your work to Figure 10.6. How does your title animation look? Are there any jitters? Does everything show up the way you intended? Are there any overlaps or obvious problems? If everything looks good, you're ready to publish. To do so, open the File menu, choose Publish Settings, and make sure you have the Flash SWF file checkbox selected. If you want to see what the differences between the other file types are, you can also publish as an HTML page with embedded SWF file or as

Figure 10.6
The Short Tragic Fall of Humpty Dumpty.

an animated GIF. You can adjust the settings of each by flipping to its tab in the Publish Settings dialog box. When you are ready, click the Publish button. (Note that to update the site at a later time, you can simply choose File > Publish; Flash will remember your previous publish settings.) Try out your finished movie. You are now ready to place your movie on a web page and share it with your friends!

Review

You have successfully completed your first animated movie. With what you've learned here, you are ready to animate slews more! Take the characters you started doodling at the start of this book and look for ways to make their stories come alive in Flash. In this chapter, you learned how to create backgrounds, add nested movie clips, add sound effects, and design transitions between scenes, which you explored by adding a title animation. In the next chapter, you'll review web design so that you can start putting your content on the World Wide Web.

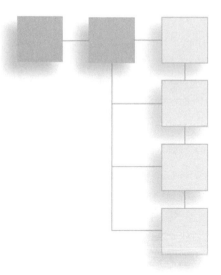

CHAPTER 11

Spinning a Web

You could design comics, cartoons, and animated characters day and night, but unless you work for a company that pays you to do just that, your work won't be seen by the world unless you self-publish. These days, easiest way to self-publish is to build a website and put your art on it, and get people to come to your website to see it—something that anybody can do for little or no cost. In this chapter, you will learn what it takes to build a website, put your work on it, and spread the word in order to get people to see your work.

A Look at the World Wide Web

There's no question that the Internet has profoundly changed our society. These days, people from all over the world chat over the World Wide Web, instantaneously sharing information in ways humanity never considered possible before the birth of the web. In this day and age, "I found it online," has become a household refrain.

As with any type of technology, understanding the history of the Internet and the underpinnings of how it works can help you to use it. Whether you're an avid web user or someone who has never bothered to "plug in," you'll need to learn a bit about the inner workings of the web before you put your comics and webtoons online.

What Is the Internet?

The Internet is a global network of computers that enables people around the world to share information. Whereas the word *intranet* denotes a private network, the word *Internet*—with a capital I—is a global network of networks, and it is growing on a daily basis.

What Are Protocols?

Although users around the world have different types of computers and operating systems (OSes), the Internet enables them to share information through the use of protocols. *Protocols* are common sets of rules that determine how computers communicate with each other over networks. For instance, each computer that is connected to the Internet connects using Transmission Control Protocol/Internet Protocol (TCP/IP).

A (Very) Brief History of the Internet

When the Soviets launched Sputnik, the first space satellite, in 1957, the U.S. government responded by instigating an aggressive campaign to stay ahead of its global competitor; hence, the Advanced Research Projects Agency (ARPA), the U.S. agency in charge of space and strategic missile research, was born. Among other things, ARPA created the first indestructible computer network, connecting computers, then housed in universities and government agencies, to prevent the destruction of important data in the event of an attack on the United States. (As an aside, the computers then in existence were giant mainframes—the kind that took up entire rooms. The small personal computer that is ubiquitous today would not arrive for several years.) This network served as a precursor to ARPANET, the first glimmer of what would become the Internet, which was born in 1969.

So What About the World Wide Web?

Many people use the terms interchangeably, but the Internet and the World Wide Web are not one and the same. The World Wide Web (WWW), often referred to as simply the web, is actually a subset of the Internet that supports *web pages,* or specially formatted documents created using languages such as Hypertext Markup Language (HTML). *Hypertext* allows you to click words in a document that are linked to related words, graphics, or other elements in the same or in another document. Put another way, you might think of the Internet as the connection between various computers worldwide, and the World Wide

Figure 11.1
Sir Tim Berners-Lee, credited with inventing the web.

Web as the content that resides on those computers that is transmitted via these connections.

Sir Tim Berners-Lee (see Figure 11.1) is often credited with the invention of the web. In 1990, while working for the Conseil Européen pour la Recherche Nucléaire (CERN), a nuclear-research facility in Switzerland that was then the largest Internet node in Europe, Berners-Lee, along with fellow CERN employee Robert Caillaiu, proposed that HTML, a language that he himself helped to develop, be used in conjunction with certain web protocols. This would enable computer users from all over the world to view information encoded in HTML from their own computers, regardless of where that information was stored. In addition to this proposal, Berners-Lee is also known to have built both the first web browser, used to display HTML documents in a human-readable format, and the first web server, used to send HTML documents to other computers. (You'll learn more about web browsers and web servers in a bit.) From Berners-Lee's work, the World Wide Web eventually emerged.

Getting Connected

In order to maintain your own web comic, you'll of course need a computer, and you'll need that computer to be connected to the Internet. That means you'll need an Internet service provider (ISP). These providers offer connections of varying types, including the following:

- Dial-up, using a telephone line and modem (generally horrifically slow)

- Digital Subscriber Line (DSL), using a telephone line and DSL modem

- Cable, available anywhere cable TV is offered

- Fixed wireless, using either satellite or microwave technologies

- Mobile wireless, using cell phone or wireless fidelity (Wi-Fi) technologies

Often your personal circumstances will dictate which option is best for you. Before picking an Internet connection, you must do your homework and check speed as well as pricing.

If you don't have your own personal computer with access to the Internet, you can use the Internet connections provided for public access in places like libraries, colleges, and universities. Although certain restrictions may apply, computers in these places are typically available for use by the general public. Even if you do have your own computer with Internet access, it's nice to know these public computers exist. For example, you might use them to update your web pages if your home machine is out of commission.

Web Speak: Know the Lingo

Just as terms like the Internet and the World Wide Web run together after a while, so do terms like web pages and websites. You'll make the distinction between these and other terms. Websites, web pages, and home pages are not alike. Take a look at the following distinctions:

- **Websites.** A *website* is a location out on the World Wide Web. For instance, http://www.msn.com is a website.

- **Web pages.** A website consists of two or more web pages. A *web page* is simply a document found on the World Wide Web, residing at a website.

- **Home pages.** A *home page* is the first web page you see when you enter a website, and it is often referred to as the *index.*

In addition to these terms, you'll want to be familiar with a few others, including the following:

- Web browser

- Web server

- IP address

- Domain

- Subdomain

- URL

- Portal

- Search engine

- Metasearch engine

Web Browsers

A *web browser* is a software program that is used to locate and display web pages. More than likely you've heard about or even used some of the most popular web browsers, like Internet Explorer, Mozilla Firefox, and Netscape Navigator. All these browsers can display graphics in addition to text. Additionally, they can display sound and video, although many require plug-ins in order for these features to work correctly. For instance, you may have noticed on sites like http://www.newgrounds.com that a plug-in called Adobe Flash Player is required to display games and videos; you must download this plug-in for your browser to play the media correctly.

Note

> It's a good idea to find all you can about the various browsers when deciding which one to use. Even more importantly, you must design your web pages to show up correctly and efficiently on all browsers, every time. This is called *cross-browser compatibility.*

Web Servers

It all seems very simple. You click, and a new page appears on your screen. But where do these pages live while they're not being looked at? Where are sites stored? Websites and the pages they contain are stored on special computers called web servers. A *web server* is a computer that is hooked up to the Internet 24/7. A web server might have one or more websites stored on it at any given time; the number of sites and pages that can reside on a server depends on the server's memory capacity. When you enter a web page address in the Address bar of your web browser, the web server responds by sending a copy of that page to your browser.

Addresses and Domains

In order for a browser to locate web pages, it must know the page's IP address, domain name, and URL.

The IP Address

An *Internet Protocol (IP) address* is a number that uniquely identifies any machine connected to the Internet, including computers, printers, and mobile devices. IP addresses can be static or dynamic. If you log in to the Internet via a broadband connection, you probably have a static IP address—one that never changes. But if you load on by way of dial-up, your ISP most likely assigns you a temporary or dynamic IP address for the amount of time you are connected.

The Domain

IP addresses consist of four groups of numbers separated by periods, such as 168.212.226.20. Because you can't be expected to remember a series of digits like this, domain names were created. A *domain name* is a text alias for one or more IP addresses. An example of a domain name is microsoft.com; you type this into your web browser instead of the IP address for Microsoft's web server.

According to Weboepedia, "because the Internet is based on IP addresses, not domain names, every web server requires a Domain Name System (DNS) server to translate domain names into IP addresses." A Domain Name System (DNS) server is separate from the web server; therefore, when you put up a new site on the World Wide Web, you must find both a web server to host your web pages and a DNS service to host your domain name. This ensures that the domain name is resolved to an IP address directed at your web server. You'll learn how to obtain a domain name and a web host in a moment.

Top-Level Domains

The ".com" part of a domain is an example of a "top-level domain." A top-level domain is an abbreviation at the end of a domain name that identifies the type of organization associated with that domain. Of course, not all domain names end in .com; here's a short list of top-level domains and the type of organization associated with each one:

- **.com.** Commercial firms, businesses, and private sites

- **.edu.** Educational institutions

- **.org.** Non-profit organizations

- **.gov.** Government agencies

- **.net.** Originally for network infrastructures, but now unrestricted

- **.mil.** Military groups

The URL

Each web page—even a page deep within a site—has its own unique uniform resource locator (URL) address. This URL is composed of the protocol used to access the page (for example, http), the domain, and possibly the folder in which the page is stored on the web server. To get a handle on this, take a look at the anatomy of a URL. Following is the URL of a page; the page itself is shown in Figure 11.2.

Figure 11.2
The web page at http:// inverloch.seraph-inn.com/viewcomic.php?page=10.

http://inverloch.seraph-inn.com/viewcomic.php?page=10

- The http:// portion of the URL is the protocol. Another protocol you might see is ftp://, used for file transferring.

- The www portion indicates that the page resides on the World Wide Web.

- The domain name, inverloch.seraph-inn.com, comes next. The period between inverloch and seraph-inn.com indicates that inverloch is a sub-site of seraph-inn.com. The .com tells you that this is either a business-related or private site.

- The third part of this URL indicates the folder in which this page is stored as well as the page name. These usually end in .htm or .html if they were designed with Hypertext Markup Language or with .xml if Extensible Markup Language was used. Here, however, you see a .php; PHP is a Hypertext Preprocessor, a scripting language widely used for dynamic web development that can be embedded into HTML. You also see a request for code from a separate page, labeled simply 10, to be displayed.

Getting a Domain Name

As mentioned, domain names are text aliases for IP addresses, making it easier for people to remember how to access a particular web page. When you are ready to build your website, one of your first steps will be to obtain a domain name for it. To get a domain name, you use an online domain name service. Some more-popular services at the time of this writing are as follows:

- **Dotster** (http://www.dotster.com)

- **GoDaddy** (http://www.godaddy.com)

- **MyDomain.com** (http://www.mydomain.com)

- **Register.com** (http://www.register.com)

N o t e

Occasionally, you will find companies that will both host your website and provide you with a domain name that is cheap or free. What usually happens is that they ask you what your want your site to be called, and then they add their own domain after it—for example, http:// creamybeamy.comicgenesis.com. If you don't mind advertising your web host in your domain name, this can be a good option. Then there are free URL redirection hosts like Dot TK (http:// www.dot.tk) that allow you to rename a long or conflicting web address for no cost, so if you have an embarrassing URL you can replace it.

Web Hosting

In addition to obtaining a domain name for your website, you will also need to obtain an account with a web host. There are countless choices; some are free, and others cost. Following is a list of free web-host services:

- **110MB** (http://110mb.com)

- **50Webs** (http://www.50webs.com)

- **AtSpace** (http://www.atspace.com)

- **Byethost** (http://www.byethost.com)

- **FreeHostia** (http://freehostia.com/free_hosting.html)

- **FreeWebs** (http://freewebs.com)

- **GeoCities** (http://geocities.com)

- **Jumpline** (http://www.jumpline.com)

- **Tripod** (http://www.tripod.com)

When choosing free hosting, go with a reputable host. Some free hosting sites add bulky code to your page, which increases the loading time or speed at which your page displays. Others place advertisements on your page or even program code that can download scripts to your visitor's computer, infecting them with spyware. Avoid these types of hosts if you can.

N o t e

Spyware is not a virus but it can be just as destructive, loading the infected computer down with random pop-ups, changing the start page on the browser, and communicating to a third party about the user's computer habits.

Companies with dedicated web servers will cost you, but as in everything else in life, you get what you pay for. The top web hosts at the time of this writing are listed here:

- **BlueHost** (http://www.bluehost.com)

- **Dot5 Hosting** (http://www.dot5hosting.com/dot5/index.bml)

- **Hosting Department** (http://www.hostingdepartment.com)

- **HostMonster** (http://www.hostmonster.com)

- **HostPapa** (http://hostpapa.com)

- **InMotion Hosting** (http://www.inmotionhosting.com)

- **StartLogic** (http://www.startlogic.com)

Some web hosts are dedicated solely to web comics. These hosts can be a boon to someone just starting out because they offer a domain name, a place to host your work, and free linking and advertisement for your site. One of the largest of these is Comic Genesis, formerly Keenspace (http://www.comicgenesis.com). Others include the following:

- **Smack Jeeves** (http://www.smackjeeves.com)

- **The Web Comic List and Fluent** (http://www.thewebcomiclist.com/fluent.php)

- **Transplant Comics** (http://transplantcomics.com)

- **Web Comics Nation** (http://www.webcomicsnation.com)

Building Your Website

Think of your website as a container. In that container, you'll need to put stuff, or content. You'll want to have a good idea of what kind of stuff, as well as how much stuff, you'll be putting in your container before you build the container; that way, you'll know what kind of container you need and how big it should be. After all, just as you wouldn't put glass marbles in a metal pan to carry them a long way, and you wouldn't put feathers in a fish-net sack, you won't want to create an enormous site for just a bit of content or vice versa. So before you get carried away with "I want! I want!" consider your content and your message to determine what you really *need*.

Does your website contain a lot of text? Is it going to be mostly images? Does it contain an equal mixture of the two? How often do you think you will be updating your site? Daily? Weekly? Monthly? Never? Answering questions like these will help you determine what kind of website you need. If you plan to build the site and never touch it again, a static site that looks really good but might be harder to edit is right for you. If you want to update it daily or weekly, you may need a blog-style site that may appear plain but can be edited in a matter of minutes. Of course, given the right tools and know-how, you can find the compromise that works best for your situation.

The following sections provide a brief primer for web development. If you decide you really want to publish your comics on the web, there are whole books dedicated to that topic that you should read. A few I'd suggest from Cengage Learning include the following:

- *Web Design for Teens* by Maneesh Sethi
- *Principles of Web Design, 4th Edition,* by Joel Sklar
- *Web Design BASICS* by Todd Stubbs and Karl Barksdale
- *PHP for Teens* by Maneesh Sethi

Preparing Images

Obviously, your web-comic site will make frequent use of images. Note that these images must be small enough for transmission over the Internet. (When I say "small," I'm referring to the size of the image file, not the dimensions of the image itself.) Unlike images you prepare for print, which must have a resolution of 150 to 300 dots per inch (dpi), an image bound for the web needs to have a resolution of 72 dpi with a file size of 200 kilobytes (KB) or less. In order to achieve this file size, you will likely need to compress your images; this reduces redundancy in image data, often without a noticeable loss in image quality. Compressing your images not only makes it more convenient for you to upload them to the web, it also benefits your visitors because it enables your website to load more quickly, displaying your graphics almost as soon as the text appears.

There are three types of widely supported images on the World Wide Web:

- **JPEG.** JPEG (pronounced *jay-peg*), short for Joint Photograhic Experts Group, is among the most common image-compression formats available.

- **GIF.** The Graphics Interchange Format (GIF) is an eight-bit-per-pixel bitmap format that supports alpha transparencies. You can pronounce GIF with a hard or soft "G" sound.

- **PNG.** Short for Portable Network Graphics, the PNG (pronounced "ping") format is a bitmapped image system with 24-bit RGB colors and improvements over GIF. PNG is great for creating low-sized files with excellent quality.

The differences between these three image types are marginal. Typically, comic artists just choose the one that suits their work the best.

Note

To save and compress your images, Adobe Photoshop comes with a built-in compression utility. To use it, open the File menu and choose Save for Web; this opens the Save for Web dialog box. Here you can choose from among the JPEG, GIF, and PNG formats, and you can preview the image while adjusting the quality settings to your satisfaction. You can also preview the image's final file size (in the bottom-left corner of the dialog box).

Preparing Text

Before you build your site or update it with new material, take time to write all your web-comic text beforehand. Your best bet is to use a word-processing program; I like Microsoft Word. It enables you to check your spelling and it even makes suggestions relating to grammar and usage. You can right-click words to view your options, including other spellings, word choices, and synonyms. This both simplifies the process of writing and double-checking your work and speeds it up. In addition, writing things out beforehand helps you ensure that you're conveying the message you want to convey on your web page without being distracted by any coding or technical aspects that are sure to crop up later.

Preparing Animations

If you've created short toons to put on the web using Flash or another 2D animation program, then the programs themselves have built-in optimization settings for your output product. If you stuck with reusable symbols and you used vector art for most of them, then file size should not be an issue. Keep in mind, however, that animation files are typically larger than static images, meaning that the download time for animation files will be longer.

Tip

Your audience will need to have to have an Adobe Flash player installed to see your Flash animations. Many people do have a Flash player, but some don't; for this reason, you should place links on your web page that enable site visitors to install Adobe Flash Player if needed. The link at the time of this writing is http://www.adobe.com/products/flashplayer.

Note

Some programs, like Eltima's Flash Optimizer (http://www.show-kit.com/flash-optimizer), promise to reduce the size of your Flash movie files by 50 percent or more—which can be a boon if you're worried about a large file size or download times.

Building and Maintaining Your Site

Adobe Dreamweaver is the premier website-construction kit for professionals. It allows pros to work in either a WYSIWYG (what-you-see-is-what-you-get) or code environment—or in both simultaneously. Dreamweaver, created primarily for users who have purchased server space online and own their own domain name, comes with several built-in site templates; all you need to do is add your content and create your custom logo. In addition, there are many free templates available online. Note that Dreamweaver can be fairly complicated; if you decide to use it to build your site but are unfamiliar with the software, you will want to have handy some resources to help you navigate the program. If you are using CS3, I suggest you read *Adobe Dreamweaver CS3 Revealed* by Sherry Bishop from Cengage Delmar Learning, 2007. Additionally, you can learn more about Dreamweaver on Adobe's site at http://www.adobe.com/products/dreamweaver/.

Another site-creation tool is Microsoft FrontPage—although it is being rapidly replaced by Microsoft's new website-authoring program, Expression. Indeed, there is a growing community of Expression users. Microsoft Expression's goal is to overtake Dreamweaver and to overcome the limitations of FrontPage with a more viable alternative. Expression is most compatible with Windows XP and Windows Vista. You can learn more about Expression on Microsoft's site at http://www.microsoft.com/expression/.

Another alternative, especially if you don't have the budget for Dreamweaver or Expression, is Nvu (pronounced "N-view"), available online at http://

```
<!DOCTYPE html PUBLI
<html>
<!-- created 2003-12-12-->
  <head><title>XYZ</title>
  </head>
  <body>
  <p>
   voluptatem accusantium do
   totam rem aperiam eaque
  </p>
  </body>
  </html>
```

HTML

Figure 11.3
Hypertext Markup Language has a very unified look.

www.nvu.com. Nvu is an open-source web-authoring application for Windows, Mac, and Linux users. This free program provides a great WYSIWYG editing environment and built-in file transfer system to satisfy most designers' needs. If you've always wanted to get your feet wet building websites, but don't have much in the way of disposable income, consider Nvu.

HTML and Hand-Coding

You are not required to use a web-authoring program such as Dreamweaver to build your site; if you prefer, you can hand-code it using HTML. HTML (see Figure 11.3) is a simple markup language that tells the browser how to display the content on the page. It's so simple, in fact, that anyone can learn to do it. Even better, the language is fairly tolerant of imperfect code—meaning you don't have to code everything just so to achieve great results. There are numerous HTML tutorials online that can get you up to speed with hand-coding in no time. To find them, search Google for "HTML tutorial" or visit http://www.pageresource.com/html/index2.htm. Note that you don't need special software to hand-code web pages in HTML; you can use a text editor such as Notepad (Win) or BBEdit (Mac) to type your code and then save your files with the .html extension. When you open them later, they'll launch in your default web browser.

Using Cascading Style Sheets

Cascading style sheets (CSS) is a computer language used to describe the presentation of structured documents that declares how a document written in a markup language such as HTML or XHTML (Extensible Hypertext Markup Language) should look. CSS (see Figure 11.4) is used to identify colors, fonts,

```
h1 { color: white;
  background: orange;
  border: 1px solid blac
  padding: 0 0 0 0;
  font-weight: bold;
}
/* begin: seaside-theme */

body {
  background-color:white;
  color:black;
  font-family:Arial,sans-serif;
  margin: 0 4px 0 0;
  border: 12px solid;
}
```

Figure 11.4
Cascading style sheets differ widely and define the look of the document without altering the content.

layout, and other notable aspects of web document staging. It is designed to facilitate the division of content and presentation of that content so that you can actually swap out different looks without changing the content. CSS is thus separate from the HTML/XHTML page coding. CSS is supported in Adobe Dreamweaver, but it can be hand-coded in Notepad or BBEdit in the same manner as the markup language.

Design Do's and Don'ts

Of course, web design is by nature a creative activity. That's not to say, however, that there aren't some basic rules that will help you develop the best site possible. Here are the most important tips I can give you to help you design your very best web pages:

- When you surf pages online, the items at the very top of a page and off to the left and right are usually noticed the least. Most web pages have advertisements, navigation links, or other information there; as a result, as a result of our web use, our brains have become programmed to ignore those areas on web pages. Don't put images and content there that you want to be seen; instead, put them dead-center in the middle of the page.

- Don't use clashing fonts and colors in your text. A sure sign of amateur web design is when the text contains multiple fonts—especially a mix of serif and sans-serif fonts (egads!)—and bright, clashing colors like pink, yellow, or blue. To give your reader a sense of simplicity, cohesion, and artfulness when they come to your website, use one font throughout your web pages, and make sure to use harmonious colors.

■ Employ a clean, interconnected design that blends well throughout all the pages on your site. You don't want your visitors thinking they've left your site when they click a link to one of your interior pages and it doesn't mesh with the page they just left; they might shrug and go away—and you don't want that.

■ Don't use competing graphics. If your artwork—your comic art or webtoons—is struggling to be seen because it's buried under opposing images and too-powerful secondary art, you will lose your audience because visitors won't know what they're supposed to look at first.

Uploading Your Files

When you obtain your domain name and web host, keep *everything*—all passwords, IP addresses, host names, and anything else connected to your website. Write it all down in a notebook and put it somewhere safe so that you don't lose it. Otherwise, you might well lose access to your site and have to perform some complicated operation to restore access. You'll need all this information whenever you edit your pages or upload your files to the web via the File Transfer Protocol (FTP).

Note

FTP allows you to upload and download files to and from the server. If you have a web-authoring program, such as Dreamweaver, you may be able to use FTP from within the program to communicate with the server. Other programs, such as SmartFTP or CuteFTP, can be used to upload files you code by hand.

Posting Your Content on Blogs and in Online Communities

Do you keep a blog or a MySpace page? Both are reputable ways to get your comics noticed. You don't have to know anything about coding, and the blog or MySpace editors are nowhere near as complicated as Adobe Dreamweaver. You can also host Flash videos, including webtoons and games, on many of these types of sites. The biggest problem is getting them noticed by search engines in order to corral people to your work. Nonetheless, this is one viable way to start distributing your comic art online, and it doesn't require you to learn a markup language or pay for server hosting and domain names.

Getting Noticed

Now that you've gotten some real estate in cyberspace and you're confident in your overall design abilities—that is, you believe people will enjoy visiting your site and reading or watching your toons—then it's time to open the doors wide and let people in. Your first step is to submit your new site to search engines so that it can be indexed.

Pages are published to the World Wide Web by their domain owners or by contributors—and just as easily, they can be changed or taken off the site. Thus, a page may be there one week and gone the next. This makes the web an ever-shifting environment. Humans can compile directories of web links that point to subjects of interest, but if these same people don't check up on their links, they may quickly become dead ends—and nothing spells a dusty site like a bunch of dead links. This is why we've developed other methods for searching the World Wide Web for the content we want: search engines and metasearch engines.

Search Tools

If you know exactly what website you want to visit, you can simply type its URL into your browser's Address bar. If not—if, for example, you know the information you seek is out there somewhere, but you're not sure where to find it—you can conduct an online search. Recent years have seen a proliferation of search tools, including the following:

- **Search engine.** A *search engine* is a program that searches the web for specified keywords and returns a list of documents in which those keywords are found. Popular search engines include Google, MSN, Yahoo!, AOL, Alta Vista, Dogpile, and Ask.com. A search engine is composed of three parts: a *spider* or *crawler,* which "crawls" through all the websites for keyword traces; an index of sites containing those keywords; and a search algorithm that makes it all happen. How the results are arranged and ranked varies by engine, although most try to put what they determine to be the most relevant and authentic results near the top of the list.

- **Metasearch engine.** *Metasearch engines* like Vivisimo and Metacrawler do not actually crawl the web to build their listings. Instead, they send the search info to multiple search engines at once and then compile their results. This can speed up your searches.

Search-Engine Optimization

Search-engine optimization (*SEO*) is the method by which web designers make websites more visible to search engines, therefore getting more people to come to their web pages. I'll show you some simple ways to add search-engine optimization to your pages later in this chapter.

Following is a list of search engines to which you should consider submitting your site:

- **AOL Search.** Locate the appropriate category and follow the onscreen instructions to submit your site.

- **AltaVista.** Visit http://addurl.altavista.com/sites/addurl/newurl and follow the onscreen instructions.

- **AskJeeves.** E-mail your site's URL, along with a description, to url@askjeeves.com.

- **Google.** Visit http://www.google.com/addurl.html and follow the onscreen instructions.

- **Hotbot.** Visit http://hotbot.lycos.com/addurl.asp and follow the onscreen instructions.

- **Lycos.** Visit http://www.lycos.com/addasite.html or http.//www.alltheweb.com/add_url.php and follow the onscreen instructions.

- **MSN Live Search.** Visit http://search.msn.com/docs/submit.aspx.

- **Open Directory Project (ODP).** Locate the appropriate category and follow the onscreen instructions to submit your site.

- **Yahoo!.** Locate the appropriate category and follow the onscreen instructions to submit your site.

In addition to submitting your site to search engines, it's also a good idea to employ search engine optimization (SEO) techniques. Although each search engine employs a different search algorithm, most are partial to scripted HTML meta content—namely descriptions, unique page titles, long-tail keywords, keywords, and keywords used in the body. For an example, take the following:

```
<head>
 <meta name="KEYWORDS" content="Drow tales dark elf elves elve manga comic
```

```
webcomic underworld fantasy">
 <title>Drowtales : Moonless Age</title>
</head>
```

Long-tail keywords are entire groupings that you'd see used in a search phrase such as "coolest fantasy anime comic," while keywords are one-word descriptors like "manga." Keywords used in the meta content should also appear in the body content, and justifiably so. If you describe your site as being about "dark elves" and the text "dark elves" never shows up anywhere in your writing, then you've committed false advertisement or at the very least decreased the chances that someone who will be interested in your content has found your site.

Another important factor of SEO is linking. Most search engines grade site performance based on how many strong web links there are going out of and coming into the site. If you place a web link to Microsoft—and Microsoft links back to you—your chances at appearing in the top 20 on a search engine go way up. Find like-minded comic artists who are willing to trade links, and link to some of the larger comic indexes (listed in Chapter 1, "So You Want to Be a Comic Artist . . .") while getting your link added to their site.

Spotlight on Sarah Ellerton

Sarah is a Unix/Windows systems administrator in Australia and a self-confessed computer geek with a passion for games, comics, and drawing. In the late 1990s Sarah showcased her *Wheel of Time* and *Final Fantasy* fan art online. Later she created her own characters and stories, and thus was born one of the largest and most colorful web comics today: *Inverloch*. The story of *Inverloch* centers around a young man named Acheron, from a horned wolf-like race called the da'kor. After a chance encounter with an elf, he finds himself on a mission, trying to locate Kayn'dar, another elf who's been missing for the past 12 years (see Figure 11.5). Making friends along the way, Acheron quickly learns that the world is not the peaceful place he believed it to be—that it is truly embroiled with prejudice, racial segregation, and hidden danger. You can read more about *Inverloch* (as well as Sarah's other projects) online at www.seraph-inn.com.

Q: At what age did you get started drawing?

A: I've always drawn casually, but I started it as a more serious hobby at about 18.

Q: What inspires you?

A: I seem to take inspiration from everything, whether that is movies, TV, games, books, other comics, or day-to-day events taking place around me. All of these things can plant the seed of an idea, which grows and evolves. Whenever I see other beautiful art, this is also an inspiration, especially to improve myself.

Q: Any beginning-artist tips?

Figure 11.5
Inverloch. (Image courtesy Sarah Ellerton, 2007.)

A: Don't make the mistake of thinking tools make the artist. It doesn't matter what you use as long as you have the passion to put your ideas forth into something more tangible. Be creative, be interesting, but most of all, love what you do. Art isn't fun and rewarding if it's a chore. Also, don't neglect the basics. Even if you're drawing in a heavily comical style, it's important to know how people, animals, and the environment are constructed. A solid foundation will make your work easier in the long run.

Q: What's the coolest thing about being a comic artist?

A: By far, the fans! It's an honor to be able to touch the lives of so many people, and hearing them say "thank you for what you've created" is simply amazing. It's not about feeling popular or making money or seeing your books on the shelves. It's about doing something for other people, about knowing you've given them something they look forward to and enjoy.

Q: Any other advice for young artists?

A: Never give up. Nobody becomes a brilliant artist overnight; it takes practice, yes, but I think first and foremost it requires dedication. Give yourself lots of small goals, and work towards them. Don't be afraid of criticism; we're only human, it hurts us all. You don't have to listen to everyone's advice. But the biggest mistake you can make is to ignore it completely.

Review

In this chapter, you learned about how the Internet and the World Wide Web (WWW) work, what the difference is between websites and web pages, and how web pages are created using markup language, cascading style sheets (CSS), and software applications such as Adobe Dreamweaver. I also showed you what you should do and what you should avoid when it comes to web design, and given you several alternatives for putting your content out there in cyberspace. Lastly, I showed you some tricks to getting your site visited on a regular basis. Now you're ready to cash in on your newfound talents!

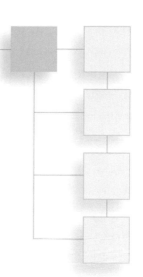

CHAPTER 12

MAKING MONEY WITH YOUR COMICS

Every artist wonders, How much is my work worth? How much am *I* worth? How much money do I need to get by? How much should I be earning? Indeed, thoughts of money are ever present—and only become more so as you grow older and wiser. Many artists, however, have no idea how to turn their art into cash. They believe that opportunities will magically appear for them "someday."

But the truth is that although most popular artists, including the ones you idolize, may have taken advantage of the occasional lucky accident, most wanted to succeed as comic artists so badly, they would go to any lengths. Likewise, you must be creative, clever, and inventive to create your own opportunities, not to mention gain the appropriate business smarts and money-matters know-how. This chapter not only shows you how other comic artists make money off their art, it also illustrates how you can develop the necessary business and financial intelligence to make something of yourself as a comic artist.

Note

Some artists attach a stigma to the notion of prosperity. These so-called "starving artists" sacrifice themselves for their art, identifying themselves as "martyrs for the cause" and their artwork as a "labor of love." In the event these artists do strike gold with their work, they are often consumed with unfounded guilt. Still other artists have been impoverished for so long that when the green stuff does finally start rolling in, they spend it as quickly as humanly possible. Establishing a sensible and healthy understanding of money is critical to your success as a web-comic artist.

Making Money with the Web

If you want your comic to be the job that feeds you, you are going to have to treat it like one. Instead of having a regular job, you're going to sit down at your art desk or computer and put in ample work every day. You can't let it slide. You will have to post regularly on your website and give your readers plenty of notice if you know you'll be gone and won't be able to update your site for a while. You do this because if you disappear, so will your readers. "Suddenly there's a little more responsibility," says Aeire of *Queen of Wands* (http://www.queenofwands.net) of maintaining a web comic, "but honestly, I don't mind it, because it's responsibility for something that I love doing anyway."

Note

Too many times, artists look to their audience for validation. Courting approval of the general public does not make you a better artist, however. It only makes you a poorer one. Instead, think of your audience as clients. That way, you are no longer creating a labor of love; you are creating something that you want to make money at– and in so doing, you have to go out and find what audiences like and what they want to see and be capable yourself of delivering it to them 100% of the time. So if your desire is to make money from a quirky cartoon elf, you should study your niche market for people who like quirky cartoon elves and deliver to them the very best quirky cartoon elf you can!

Assuming you treat your web comic as a job, you can earn money in several ways, including the following:

- **Donations.** Most artists solicit donations or use "tip jars" (using PayPal, for instance)—relying on their readers' patronage.

- **Advertising or subscriptions.** If a web comic has enough traffic, advertising and/or subscription revenue can be generated.

- **Merchandising.** Some sell merchandise, such as shirts, mugs, stickers, and so on, featuring their artwork, often through online services such as CafePress. Some truly successful web comics have been redistributed in comic albums or digital videos.

Invest in Yourself

The most common finance-related mistake an artist can make is not investing in his or her own career. Although artists often spend an overwhelming amount of money on art supplies and materials, they become skimpy when it comes to other aspects of career development: presentation, fashion, publicity, mail-outs, travel, networking, and more. Creating artwork and putting it out there for everyone to see is half of your job. The other half is building and maintaining your image, getting the right people to notice you, and pulling yourself up by the bootstraps until you earn a decent wage off your art.

Donations

Unfortunately, readers who donate regularly simply because they are nice are a singular breed. And for those people who do donate, it's usually a one-time thing. That said, there *are* people who will support you, so you might as well stick a donation link on your website. Every bit helps. Just don't rely on donations as your sole source of income, especially if you don't have a stupendously large fan base.

Many artists get creative with their tip jars. There are some that say "Feed Me—I'm a Starving Artist!" (see Figure 12.1) and some that say "Support[Insert Name of Character from Comic Strip Here]." Some artists even go out of their way to say they have a cause for which they need to raise a large sum of money, such as participating in an upcoming convention or paying for Internet bandwidth. If you use this approach, determine how much your cause will cost, insert an image of a bar graph on the site that ranges from zero to the amount that you need, and

Figure 12.1
Greg Dean of *Real Life* asks for donations through PayPal on his site.

nudge the bar toward your goal as you receive donations. Readers are often more likely to donate when they see this type of graphic because it illustrates the need and how their contributions can help fulfill it.

Another strategy for obtaining donations is the pay-for-a-treat approach. It works like this: A reader donates some money to your web comic, after which you send him or her an extra morsel to which non-donating readers do not have access. These thank-you gifts can be desktop wallpaper, behind-the-scenes sketches, extra comics, Flash games, or sneak peeks at things you are currently working on.

Note

A good way to accept donations through your site is via PayPal. Note, however, that you might need your parents' help setting up a PayPal account. To initiate the setup process, go to http://www.paypal.com and click the Sign Up button.

Spotlight on Faith Erin Hicks

A Canadian artist who works for an animation studio and makes web comics in her spare time, Faith Erin Hicks is the creator of such well-known series as *Demonology 101* (see Figure 12.2), *Zombies Calling*, and *Ice*. Her distinctive characters and line style set her apart from many comic artists and have made her one of the most-linked-to comic artists today. You can see more of her work online at http://www.faitherinhicks.com.

Q. How old were you when you got started drawing?

A: I used to draw horses when I was a kid, but I don't think I really started drawing intently until I got into university. So I was probably around 18 or 19 when I started drawing. It was a late start, but I think I've made up for it by drawing way too much in the last few years!

Q: What inspires you?

A: Books and the work of other artists. I love a good novel, but my favorite thing is a well-written comic book. It's the combination of two things I love best: art and writing.

Q: Do you have any beginning-artist tips?

A: Practice as much as you can! And don't try and imitate other artists directly. You'll develop a lot better if you try and discover the kind of drawing that works best for you.

Q: What's the coolest thing about being a comic artist?

A: You get to do everything, if you want to. I get to write my comics, design the characters, plan the plot twists, and draw them. And then if someone likes what you've done, you can be really proud of the work you've created, because you did it all yourself.

"Let there be villains." -C.S. Lewis

an online comic by faith erin hicks

Demonology 101

Figure 12.2
Demonology 101. (Image courtesy Faith Erin Hicks, 2007.)

Q: Do you have any other advice for young artists?

A: If you want to draw people, I would recommend taking a life drawing course, so you can learn anatomy. Don't try and learn anatomy from a comic book. You'll only end up with a distorted (and limiting) picture of what human beings look like.

Advertising

If you have a fan base whose numbers reach into the thousands, then odds are that companies and other sites might be interested in using your site to advertise their product or service. Alternatively, you might find websites in the same category as yours that are willing to advertise on your site. Be aware, however, that advertising can negatively affect the appearance of your site, so you should exercise this option with care. Decide what kind of ads you're willing to allow and how much space you are willing to allot to advertisers.

Tip

Many web-comic sites are hosted by a company called Keenspot, which, in addition to providing convenient and reliable web hosting for online comics, also issues the comics' creators quarterly checks for allowing advertising banners on their sites. Keenspot artists get web accounts with unlimited space and bandwidth plus access to Autokeen scripts, which are utilities that automatically handle the updating and archiving of your comics. It's a nice setup because you don't have to pay for bandwidth or server costs, and you don't have to seek advertisers yourself.

Micro-payments

Scott McCloud, author of *Understanding Comics: The Invisible Art*, supports using micro-payments to fund web comics. The basic concept is that the creator of a web comic charges his or her readers between 1¢ and 25¢ per issue. Just to wrap your brain around it, imagine that you have a weekly comic that draws 25,000 readers a week. This is individual readers, not hits. If each one of your readers pays you, say, 5¢ per issue, then your yearly income would be $65,000 a year before taxes. That's more than what most people bring in working as nurses or mechanics! Although the *Modern Tales* family of sites has successfully used this subscription model, the fact is that most web-comic readers don't support this method. After all, why pay for something they could find for free elsewhere online?

Tycho Brahe of *Penny Arcade* (http://www.Penny-Arcade.com) says of Scott McCloud's micro-payment theory, "For someone like Scott McCloud, somebody who is already established in real-space media, [micro-payments] might work—but if this mechanism is chiefly of use to those already enfranchised, that takes his inspiring manifesto down a couple pegs... He imagines that other people—in fact, that everyone—would gladly pay for things if given the chance to do so." In reality, however, everyone will *not* pay for things if they don't have to. Moreover, using micro-payments may slow down the growth of your readership. A person can't say, "Hey, look at this great comic I found!" and send the link to all his or her friends without first having to convince them to spend some money. Nonetheless, you might come up with a way to make the micro-payments model work for you. For more information, check out BitPass, a company (for which McCloud serves as an advisor) that specializes in micro-payments at http://www.reg.net/bitpass.

Merchandising

Most web-comic artists who support themselves with their web comics earn the bulk of their revenue from selling comic-related merchandise. You can open an online store using PayPal to sell t-shirts, prints, mouse pads, or anything else you can think of that your readers might be interested in buying.

Tip

Before you devote a ton of time designing merchandise for sale on your site, ask your readers what they might like to buy from you. Even better, have them vote on it. Put a poll on your site. Find out what people want, and then deliver.

To avoid investing a ton of cash in your merchandise up front, not to mention spending loads of time making, sorting, and shipping your goods (not to mention handling payments), consider using a company like CafePress (see Figure 12.3) or Warehouse 23 to handle things for you. These companies take a

Figure 12.3
CafePress is one viable alternative to opening an online store.

commission out of your profits, but you won't get burdened by having to keep stock in your store. Aeire of *Queen of Wands* uses Warehouse 23 and says, "I get less of a cut off of what sells, but at the same time I don't have to worry about printing or having stock on hand or even setting up a store, which is nice."

Caution

When it comes to selling merchandise, start small. You can always add more later. For instance, you could create one design with your main character or logo on it and then put it on t-shirts available at CafePress. If people buy your t-shirts and seem to want more, you can add another product, such as a coffee mug or mouse pad with the same design on it. Over a couple of years you can start adding other designs and artwork on various new merchandise, until you realize your store has grown.

In addition to selling merchandise such as shirts, mouse pads, and the like, you should consider self-publication of your comics in book form as a means of promotion, developing a personal franchise, and sharing your work with a creative community anxious to see something new. For more information about self-publishing, see *Publishing Gems: Insider Information for the Self-Publishing Writer* by Brent Sampson.

The Law

It's not enough to have some business know-how. As a comic artist, you must know the law. There are low lifes everywhere who'd like to take advantage of artists just like you; they know they don't have the talent, so they want to make money off yours. Several rising stars in the art world have lost their work because they didn't keep their originals; instead, they gave them away to others who later published or sold them as their own. Much has changed thanks to new legislation and to changes in existing laws that protect artists from being victimized, but undoubtedly a day does not pass that some artist isn't ripped off by some opportunist.

As Tad Crawford said in his book *Legal Guide for the Visual Artist,* "Artists should never feel intimidated, helpless, or victimized. Legal and business considerations exist from the moment an artist conceives a work or receives an assignment. While no handbook can solve the unique problems of each artist, the artist's increased awareness of the general legal issues pertaining to art will aid in avoiding risks and gaining benefits that might otherwise pass unnoticed." The latest edition of Crawford's book covers issues of multimedia and digital art.

Copyright

An important legal aspect of working as an artist is copyright. Copyright protection is available to artists working in every single medium. Any artwork is protected by copyright as soon as it comes into being as long as you place a copyright notice on your work. This consists of "Copyright," "Copr.," or "©"; your name or what you are known by; and the year of the piece's creation. This form of copyright is free and fair and lasts the duration of your life plus 50 years.

Although you aren't required to formally register your copyright, there are certain advantages that mainly concern your rights if anyone infringes on your copyright. If you need more help or guidance on copyright laws, pick up Tad Crawford's book *Legal Guide for the Visual Artist*.

Contracts and Financial Records

Most artists I know use contracts when dealing with business-related clients. For instance, whenever I work with a corporate entity to design its logo or make a jazzy t-shirt design, I typically use a standard contract and invoicing system to make sure I get paid and don't get taken advantage of. Requiring the people with whom you do business to use contracts is not a sign of mistrust. In fact, it shows a degree of seriousness and credibility that most entities will find comforting, demonstrating that you take care of yourself and you treat your work as a serious matter. You also show them you want to maintain a smooth working relationship without any trip-ups. In fact, many clients insist on the use of contracts and become concerned only if you appear reticent.

Some rules apply to teens that do not apply to adults, however—especially when they involve work relationships and contractual agreements. Your parents or guardians will typically have to sign all contracts. Also, because you are a minor and a dependent listed on their tax statements, you will have to keep careful record of your financial documents, such as what you've earned and what you've spent (on your business) and give them to your parents or guardians when it comes time for them to file their tax information with the IRS.

Review

You could use any or all of the moneymaking suggestions in this chapter. Using one of the methods discussed here by itself will probably not be enough to live off of, but each little bit helps support your endeavors. You could also come up with an entirely new model for web-comic distribution. There are lots of ways you can show your teachers, parents, and friends that you can become financially successful with your drawings.

CHAPTER 13

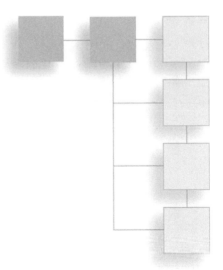

FINAL WORDS

Children have a knack, from a very young age, for drawing wacky and weird characters to amuse themselves and their friends. Somewhere along the way, on the trip to adulthood, most people lose that knack, or simply stop believing in themselves. I hope that this book has shown you how to harness that natural whimsy to ensure it doesn't disappear. The majority of hard-core cartoonists started doodling at a tender age and just never stopped. You might say they just never grew up. Nurture your nature, so that you never grow up either!

If drawing comic art and animating toons doesn't make you happy, find something else to do. Drawing isn't merely a job, and it probably won't net you the big bucks that other occupations can, so if you're going to do it, you have to love it. Drawing is a calling. If you don't have it, it will never make you happy— although you can certainly learn how to do it. If you do hear that call, however, then you might have what it takes to be a modern-day legend like Bob Kane or Stan Lee or even Walt Disney. Don't give up, continue to apply yourself, and experiment with new techniques and technology to perfect your product.

Don't remain idle, either. Get out there. Get your work on the World Wide Web for everybody to see, even if your work isn't 100% perfect. You can't wait. Also, attend as many comic conventions as possible. The two biggest comic-art conventions, held every year in San Francisco, California, are Comic-Con in

November and WonderCon in February (http://www.comic-con.org). You can find links to other conventions and a calendar of events online at http://www.comicbookconventions.com. Whether you're a fan of comics yourself or not, you are now a comic artist in your own right, and as such you have the right to show your work off. Who knows? Like Colleen Doran, you might be scouted by a comic-book publisher at one of the conventions. Or those animations that you put on your website might draw the attention of a large animation house or TV network. You won't know all the opportunities that await you unless you try!

Steve Barr, a professional cartoonist, animator, and illustrator, says, "I actually sold my first two cartoons to a magazine and a syndicated newspaper feature when I was in seventh grade! I will never forget those first two checks. One was for $7.50, the other for $25. I was elated. Someone had actually purchased my work. I had been paid for it! I was a professional. From that point on, I pursued my dream. By the time I was in high school I was having work published regularly by a variety of magazines, and even landed a job doing some black and white line illustrations for a book publisher."

All this is possible, if you are ready. I sincerely hope this book launches you into the cartoon career you've always dreamed about. If not, and if you are just wanting to make web comics for recreational purposes, that's cool too. Apply yourself and see what you can make.

The following are resources, information, and communities that you can find on the Internet to assist you in your comic-art venture. All links are valid at the time of this writing but are subject to change. If they do change—or you get a 404 error—you can typically browse for the new web address using a search engine.

Software

Listed here are links to software applications, computer tools, and whatzits that can assist your comic endeavors.

- **Adobe Dreamweaver:** http://www.adobe.com/products/dreamweaver

- **Adobe Flash:** http://www.adobe.com/products/flash

- **Adobe Photoshop:** http://www.adobe.com/products/photoshop

- **Anime Studio:** http://www.e-frontier.com

- **Audacity:** http://audacity.sourceforge.net

- **Bauhaus Mirage Studio:** http://www.bauhaussoftware.com

- **DigiCel Flipbook:** http://www.digicelinc.com

- **GIMP:** http://www.gimp.org

- **Eltima Flash Optimizer:** http://www.show-kit.com/flash-optimizer

- **Microsoft Expression:** http://www.microsoft.com/expression

- **Nvu:** http://www.nvu.com

- **Paint Dot Net:** http://www.getpaint.net

- **Toon Boom Studio:** http://www.toonboom.com

Artist Resources

Listed here are links to royalty-free graphics, tutorials, blogs, magazines, and other information for 2D artists.

- **2D Artist Magazine:** http://www.2dartistmag.com

- **Animation Meat:** http://www.animationmeat.com

- **Animation World Magazine:** http://mag.awn.com

- **ASIFA-Hollywood Animation Archive:** http://www.animationarchive.org

- **Cartoon Brew:** http://www.cartoonbrew.com

- **Cartoon Smart Flash Tutorials:** http://www.cartoonsmart.com

- **Character Design:** http://characterdesign.blogspot.com

- **Drawn! The Illustration and Cartooning Blog:** http://drawn.ca

- **Gene Deitch: How to Succeed in Animation:** http://genedeitch.awn.com

- **Morgue File:** http://www.morguefile.com

- **The Animation Podcast:** http://www.animationpodcast.com

Sound Resources

Listed here are links to sound effects and music, including compressed and uncompressed audio files, which are royalty-free.

- **Bbm.net:** http://www.bbm.net
- **DeusX.com:** http://www.deusx.com/studio.html
- **Flashkit.com:** http://www.flashkit.com
- **Flashsound.com:** http://www.flashsound.com
- **Killersound.com:** http://www.killersound.com
- **Shockwave-Sound.com:** http://shockwave-sound.com
- **Soundrangers.com:** http://www.soundrangers.com

Web Hosting and So Much More

Listed here are links to server spaces, domain name–registration services, and web stores. Some of these cost and some are free.

- **110MB:** http://110mb.com
- **50Webs:** http://www.50webs.com
- **AtSpace:** http://www.atspace.com
- **BlueHost:** http://www.bluehost.com
- **Byethost:** http://www.byethost.com
- **CafePress:** http://www.cafepress.com
- **Dot5 Hosting:** http://www.dot5hosting.com/dot5/index.bml
- **FreeHostia:** http://freehostia.com/free_hosting.html
- **FreeWebs:** http://www.freewebs.com
- **HostGator:** http://www.hostgator.com
- **Hosting Department:** http://www.hostingdepartment.net

- **HostMonster:** http://www.hostmonster.com

- **HostPapa:** http://hostpapa.com

- **InMotion Hosting:** http://www.inmotionhosting.com

- **Jumpline:** http://www.jumpline.com

- **StartLogic:** http://www.startlogic.com

- **The Web Comic List and Fluent:** http://www.thewebcomiclist.com/fluent.php

- **Warehouse 23:** http://www.warehouse23.com

Comic Indexes and Hosting Sites

Listed here are links to web-comic directories, webtoon indexes, and comic hosting sites. You can either put your comic art on their pages or have them link to your work.

- **Comic Genesis:** http://www.comicgenesis.com

- **Comics at Six Killer Bunnies:** http://sixkillerbunnies.com/comicsindex

- **Comics.com:** http://www.comics.com

- **Comixpedia:** http://www.comixpedia.org

- **Keenspot:** http://www.keenspot.com

- **MyToons Animation:** http://www.mytoons.com

- **Online Comics:** http://www.onlinecomics.net

- **Smack Jeeves:** http://www.smackjeeves.com

- **The Webcomic List:** http://www.thewebcomiclist.com

- **TopWebComics.com:** http://topwebcomics.com

- **Transplant Comics:** http://transplantcomics.com

- **Web Comic Hottness:** http://www.puddlejumpart.com/thehotness

- **Web Comics Nation:** http://www.webcomicsnation.com

- **Webcomics.com:** http://webcomics.com

- **Wikipedia's List of Web Comics:** http://en.wikipedia.org/wiki/List_of_webcomics

Artists Spotlighted in This Book

Following are the sites of the comic artists and animators who volunteered their time and contributed their work for this book. I couldn't have done it without them!

- **Esrix:** http://www.entity.comicgen.com

- **Faith Erin Hicks:** http://www.faitherinhicks.com

- **James Farr:** http://www.xombified.com

- **Jason "Hot Lips" Yungbluth:** http://www.whatisdeepfried.com

- **Robert and Margaret Carspecken:** http://www.ozfoxes.com

- **Sarah Ellerton:** http://www.seraph-inn.com

Review

In this book, you learned the history of comics, web comics, and animation, plus the taxonomy used for each. You learned how to draw objects out of basic shapes and how to make compelling characters. You learned how to write heroic stories and gag strips, and how to set up a web comic as well as how to animate a webtoon in Adobe Flash. You learned how to display your artwork on the World Wide Web and get people to notice it. You know how to make money off your endeavors and what to watch out for when negotiating with clients in the art world. You have, in fact, discovered everything there is to know about making web comics and animations; anything still left to be discovered, you are now adequately equipped to pick up. All that is left is for you to get to work! Good luck.

APPENDIX

The following are examples of gag strips and comic pages from the art desk of Michael Duggan. For more artwork, see http://www.mdduggan.com.

INDEX

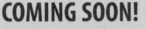

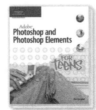